LOST ADDRESSES

LOST ADDRESSES

A MEMOIR OF INDIA 1934–1955

KRISHNA BOSE

TRANSLATED FROM BENGALI BY
Sumantra Bose

NIYOGI BOOKS

First published in Bengali as
Harano Thikana by Ananda Publishers in 2013.

Published by
NIYOGI BOOKS
D-78, Okhla Industrial Area, Phase-I
New Delhi-110 020, INDIA
Tel: 91-11-26816301, 49327000
Fax: 91-11-26810483, 26813830
email: niyogibooks@gmail.com
website: www.niyogibooksindia.com

Editor: Sucharita Ghosh
Cover Design: Dsgn Unplugged
Design: Shashi Bhushan Prasad

ISBN: 978-93-85285-06-6
Publication: 2015

Printed at: Niyogi Offset Pvt. Ltd., New Delhi, India

IN RESPECTFUL REMEMBRANCE OF MY
FATHER CHARU CHANDRA CHAUDHURI
(1895–1987)

CONTENTS

TRANSLATOR'S NOTE

This is my first work of translation. I must say I have enjoyed doing it a great deal.

It's been especially satisfying to translate a work published in my own language, Bengali, into the language in which I write my own work, English.

The book I have translated is distinguished by the simplicity of its style of expression. The language is free-flowing and makes for a delightful read. At the same time, it is crafted in elegant Bengali. The simplicity and the elegance are woven together seamlessly. There are occasional passages which are almost lyrical, and they fit well into the book, enriching rather than disturbing the way the story is told. My translation has tried to retain the style, spirit and character of the Bengali original.

The Bengali book is a remarkable blend of the private and the public, the personal and the national. The memoir by a woman now in her eighties of the first quarter-century of her life combines the story of her immediate and extended family with a narrative of many major events in India just before and after Independence. It is not a retrospective account of those events and that time, although there are occasional reflections on how those events and that time shaped the author's later life. The public and national part of the story is told just as it was seen and experienced first by a little girl, then an adolescent and finally a young adult. This is what makes it a valuable eyewitness record of India during the last decade of the British Raj and the first decade after Independence. Whilst rooted in Bengal, the memoir travels across India—literally and otherwise—and has a pan-Indian flavour and resonance. That is why I decided to translate it, in the hope that it will interest, inform and enlighten English-reading Indians across the country, especially the younger generations.

Sumantra Bose
Kolkata and London, 9th December 2014

EARTHQUAKE

Chowringhee Road, central Calcutta, 1934. A road synonymous with the British Empire in India since the era of the East India Company. In a quiet street just off this road lined with grand colonial buildings, a middle-class Bengali family had set up home in a modest two-storeyed house. I'm not sure how we came to be there. Chowringhee was an area meant for 'Europeans'—whites. Of course, our street was at an end of Chowringhee adjoining Bhowanipur, a solidly Bengali middle-class locality. Still, we were on the wrong side of an undrawn but very real border between two Calcuttas, white and brown.

That little house off Chowringhee was my first address in life. And the site of my first memory, aged three.

The entrance of the house had two or three steps leading to the pavement. Mother was standing at the top of the steps, me holding on to her *aanchal*, the hem of her sari. She was buying *chine badam*, a peanut snack, from a passing *pheriwala*, a street vendor. Bargaining over, he was scooping our peanuts from a big bag into a *thonga*, a pocket-like container made from newspaper. Suddenly there was a commotion on the street. People started to run helter-skelter. Then the sound of conch shells rang out from nearby houses. Mother, startled, mumbled, 'There was just an earthquake, quite a strong one!'

That was the famous earthquake which struck eastern India on 15 January 1934 at about two in the afternoon. Parts of Bihar

DELICIOUS TIBETAN &

province, adjoining Bengal, were levelled and thousands were killed there. In Calcutta, the tremors were strong enough to collapse the tower of St Paul's Cathedral on Chowringhee. My problem was different. I started wailing, 'I want to see the earthquake.' But the earthquake had come and gone. That's my first ever memory: crying after the earthquake, not in fear but upset at having missed it.

My next memory is also related to the earthquake. Holding Mother's hand tight, I was riding the lift to an upper floor of Esplanade Mansions, an apartment building in the heart of central Calcutta. The ride was itself a novelty, few Calcutta buildings had lifts or elevators in those days. When we emerged, Mother pressed the doorbell of an apartment and a white woman opened the door. She was dishevelled, eyes red from crying. Mother started to comfort her. This was Aunt Anna, the American wife of her brother and my Phul mama ('Flower Uncle'), Kiran Roy. He had been on work in Darbhanga, a district of Bihar devastated by the earthquake. There was no word from him for ten days.

One of contemporary Calcutta's landmarks, the imposing marble monument called the Victoria Memorial built over the first two decades of the last century to honour Queen Victoria of Britain, was just a short walk from our house. Father and Mother disagreed on many things but they had a shared love of morning walks. The sprawling compound of the Victoria Memorial, dotted with paths through neat rows of trees and small water bodies, was an obvious choice. An Indian policeman sporting a large red turban was permanently on guard by the statue of Victoria on her throne which dominates one of the approaches to the main building. Those were the years in which revolutionary Bengali youths waged a desperate armed struggle against the British in Calcutta and across the province of Bengal. The red-turbaned guard and I soon became fast friends. I remember chattering endlessly to him. One day Father clicked a photograph of me standing in front of a tree blossoming with flowers. He named the photograph after a line from a poem by William Wordsworth—'Heaven lies about us in our infancy'.

Facing page: *The little house off Chowringhee eighty years later (October 2014)*

Our Victoria Memorial jaunts created a peculiar problem at home—in a manner of speaking. We were renting part of the house from the owners, Bengalis of an old-fashioned if not archaic mentality who lived in another part of the house. They deemed a married Indian woman taking morning walks in a public place deeply shameful, and started taunting my mother about it. It was just the three of us in that house—my parents and their only child—but I had five uncles, my father's younger brothers, living in various other parts of Calcutta. On Sundays and holidays this bunch of *kaka*s (paternal uncles) would often turn up at our place. One morning an abusive remark about my mother proved too much for one of my uncles, a typical hot-headed Bengali from East Bengal (present-day Bangladesh). He lunged at our landlord and punched him in the face. The matter reached the police and from then on our days in that house were numbered.

Mother, who was from a prominent and progressive family, also of East Bengal, was not easily cowed. She kept up the morning-walk routine. One day Father was unwell and she went by herself, me in tow. That day we encountered a different problem—a man started following her as we strolled. I encountered the same problem some years later, when I was a teenage school student in the tenth standard. I was walking my dog, Jimmy, around the picturesque lakes in the heart of residential south Calcutta when a group of boys started to follow me, chanting, 'Look at the twentieth-century girl, walking her dog on a leash.' That day in Victoria Memorial my red-turbaned friend came to our rescue. Alerted by my mother, he chased the stalker off the grounds in no time.

Later I often wondered why Mother's morning walks caused so much trouble. I think that while she was accustomed to the relatively liberal lifestyle of her family in East Bengal, parts of Calcutta society were still living in the nineteenth century.

I still vividly remember the rooms of the house off Chowringhee. One day my paternal uncles had come to visit. They were chatting with Father in his study on the ground floor. Mother was busy laying out the table in the dining room, also on the ground floor. But I was upstairs in the bedroom, with one of my uncles for company. He was painting my face with pieces of coal, and messing about with my hair. He had persuaded me to take on the persona of a *pagli* (mad woman). Make-up done, he asked me to hide behind my mother's ornate wardrobe until he gave me a signal to emerge and startle everyone. As fate would have it, Mother came upstairs and spotted me crouched behind her wardrobe in my pagli get-up. In response to her scolding I shrieked, 'But *bichhu* (scorpion) wanted me to be a pagli!'

That uncle was the oldest of my father's younger brothers, just two years junior to him. When I was a bit older I addressed him as 'Maejo kaka' ('Elder uncle'), but at that time he used to call me 'bichhu' as a term of endearment and I used to call him by the same moniker. He was to become internationally known later in his life as the writer Nirad C. Chaudhuri. And much of his writing, acerbic in tone, did resemble a scorpion's sting.

One afternoon Father was taking a nap in his armchair in our first-floor living room. Or trying to. I was on the floor by his feet, talking endlessly while playing with little brass figurines of camels, deer, peacocks, horses and other animals. We had got these during a trip to Benares. I don't remember much about our holiday in the temple town except a vague memory of monkeys scampering about everywhere. Opposite the front windows of the living room was a handsome mansion. British people lived there. We could see the massive staircase going up the middle of their house. 'Baba, I dreamed last night that a huge elephant was going up those stairs,' I informed my father. 'It was making a *thup-thup* noise as it did.' Mother came in and said, 'What rubbish. Elephants climbing stairs of houses!' Seeing my deflated face, Father solemnly said, 'Of course. It's quite possible.' The elephant talk was abruptly interrupted by the sound of a car stopping outside. Then there were footsteps on the stairs. There was a tiny balcony, open to the sky, wedged between the living room and the bedroom at the rear. My paternal grandfather, Upendra Narayan Chaudhuri, appeared on that balcony. Mother quickly pulled the aanchal of her sari over her head and bent down to touch her father-in-law's feet. That is the one image of my grandfather I retain from childhood. It's as if someone invisible said 'Cut!' right after that scene.

After my grandmother's death, my grandfather went off to Benares to spend his sunset years in solitude. Their sons were all grown and more or less secure in life, while the two daughters were married. He would visit Calcutta rarely, on special family occasions. It was not unusual in those days for elderly men like him to take up residence in Kashi (another name for Benares, present-day Varanasi), once family concerns no longer detained them.

The occasion for that visit was the marriage of my Shaejo kaka—the uncle next in age to Uncle Nirad. Shaejo kaka, Khirode Chandra Chaudhuri, was a well-known doctor, a paediatrician. I have blurry memories of the wedding. A big two-storeyed house, rented for the ceremonies, buzzing with noise and activity. A British couple living in the next house objected to the noise. An argument broke out and escalated to a fistfight between the man and my Chhoto kaka (youngest uncle). There was a complaint to the local police station but fortunately Chhoto kaka was not arrested. Had he been, he would have missed a family wedding, and not for the first time. Two years earlier Chhoto kaka, Benode Chandra Chaudhuri, had missed Uncle Nirad's wedding because he and another of my uncles, Manmatha Chandra, had been in jail after joining Mahatma Gandhi's civil disobedience movement. The duo sent best wishes to their new sister-in-law from prison. In those days such occurrences were common, as were brawls on the streets with whites.

My last memory of the house off Chowringhee is of a celebration. I was dressed in a red frilly frock made of georgette cloth bought by Father from Whiteaway Laidlaw, a premier department store of Calcutta at the time. It was my fourth birthday. It was early evening and the little house was filling up with people. Both Father and

Mother had large families. Father had five brothers and two sisters. Mother too had five brothers and two sisters. Of course, not all were resident in Calcutta. Several lived in the home country (*daesh*) in East Bengal. My father's two sisters were in Mymensingh, the district in the east their family is from. Mother's eldest brother lived in Dhaka, and one of her sisters was in Burma (Myanmar). But still there were plenty of relatives on hand. Phul mama—Uncle

LEFT: *Krishna with her parents at the age of four (1935)*

Kiran, my mother's brother—arrived. I heard his voice, 'Where's Krishnakali' (an affectionate take on my name). 'What, still not ready for the party!' He picked me up and carried me downstairs. As we came down the stairs I could hear the chatter of many people and smell the food.

The address off Chowringhee Road disappeared from my life after that.

Although I grew up in Calcutta, I was born in my maternal grandfather's house in Dhaka. In those days Indian women would typically go to their parents' house to give birth, especially to the first child. I was born ten years after my parents' marriage, so the occasion was even more special. I've been told that after all arrangements had been made for my mother's journey from Calcutta to Dhaka—by train and then by riverboat—a priest declared the day of departure inauspicious. The dilemma was resolved when he ruled that the journey could be regarded as having begun the previous night if she slept outside her bedroom.

My birth is associated with the story of a 'miracle'. Three years into her marriage Mother became pregnant but unfortunately suffered a miscarriage. After that she failed to conceive for nearly seven years. Her unhappiness at being childless was compounded by the caustic comments of some relatives. She would pray constantly for a child but the Almighty failed to oblige. Then something happened when she went on a trip to Benares to visit her father-in-law, accompanied by one of her sisters-in-law, a married woman with a son. A renowned *pundit* (man learned in religious scriptures) of the temple town decreed that Mother should offer *puja* (prayers) on a particular day and the next morning bathe in the holy Ganges, and a child would be assured. Mother duly offered prayers but the next morning she woke to find that her period had commenced, making the dip in the holy river impossible. She was crushed. At that point her sister-in-law stepped in. She told my mother that she would take the bath in the holy waters while praying that my mother's wish be fulfilled. The Almighty answered the proxy's efforts and soon after I was conceived.

Some years after the birth of Bangladesh, I visited the house in its capital where I was born. I wasn't sure that Lakshmi Bazar, once a mainly Hindu neighbourhood of Dhaka, was still there, let alone my grandfather's house. But friends in Dhaka insisted on taking me there and sure enough, both the locality and the house were there.

I had heard so many stories about that house from my mother and my grandmother. My maternal grandfather, Lalit Roy, was one of East Bengal's biggest landowners, a *zamindar*. The estate was in a rural area called Narsingdi, but they lived in Dhaka. My grandfather was a thoroughly unusual member of the zamindar class—he was a fervent and active supporter of the national struggle for freedom from British rule. Mother told me that many nights she would be woken by the harsh sound of boots marching outside and would realise that the house had been cordoned off by police for yet another search. The police's suspicions were not unfounded. My grandmother told me, 'Your grandfather would regularly wake me in the middle of the night, and ask me to quickly prepare a simple meal. I would get up and find unknown young men barely out of their teens in the house, usually two at a time. They would eat and disappear. I never saw any of them again.' These were members of the legendary revolutionary organisations of East Bengal who had taken up arms to liberate India.

At that time the motorised riverboats, known as 'launches' or 'steamers', which transported passengers and goods across East Bengal were all owned by British firms. My grandfather decided to rectify this and floated his own riverboat operation. The business didn't do well, however. As an incentive tea and biscuits began to be supplied free of charge to passengers. To no avail—passengers still seemed to prefer the British-owned ferries. He had to wind up the business. A small part of the estate had to be sold to recoup the losses.

But the failed venture did have its uses while it operated. Many underground freedom fighters would move about on the

Above: *Lalit Roy, Krishna's maternal grandfather (mid 1930s)*

Above right: *Lalit Roy (extreme right) with Subhas Chandra Bose (1938)*

riverboats in the guise of *khalasi*s (helpers). Many years later one such young man told me about his experiences—by that time, later in life, he had become a well-known monk under the name Trailokya Maharaj.

Finally the British got my grandfather. He was arrested, convicted in the celebrated 'Dacca Conspiracy Case' and sent to prison. The lawyer who represented the defendants was none other than the renowned nationalist leader Chitta Ranjan (C.R.) Das, popularly known by his honorific title *Deshbandhu* (Friend of the Nation).

My grandfather had all sorts of ways of rejecting colonialism. In those days, sons of families of high status and means would often go to England—usually to Oxford or Cambridge—for higher education. My grandfather too was keen to send his sons abroad to study but England was a no-no. So he picked the United States of

America. In the 1920s he sent his second son to study at Harvard University in Cambridge, Massachusetts. Another son went to Germany. Then yet another son, my favourite Uncle Kiran, went to the Massachusetts Institute of Technology (MIT); he met his American wife whilst studying there.

My nationalist zamindar grandfather was also heavily into social reform causes. He would especially encourage remarriage of women widowed at a young age after being married off early and he would personally arrange such remarriages. Word reached him that he was being criticised in society for foisting widows on other families' sons. So as soon as my uncle returned from Harvard, he was married to a young widow. That new aunt of mine was a talented singer.

When Phul mama (Uncle Kiran) announced that he wished to marry an American woman, my grandfather was delighted. He welcomed Aunt Anna, a Catholic by upbringing, into the family with open arms. Aunt Anna was touched and said 'thank you' to him in the Western style. Her father-in-law responded, 'We should be thanking you. You have come to this faraway land, leaving your family and friends behind, out of love for my son.'

Despite the failure of the riverboat venture, my grandfather remained committed to building *swadeshi* (national) business enterprises. My Harvard-returned uncle took the lead in building up Bengal Belting and Bengal Lamp, which were successful and important Bengali-owned firms for decades. His brothers joined him in swadeshi entrepreneurship. Many decades later I was elected to India's Parliament three times from the Jadavpur constituency covering parts of south Kolkata, its suburbs, and adjacent rural areas. My earliest memories of Jadavpur are of visiting a leafy suburb full of green fields and little ponds as a child. That was where the Bengal Lamp factory came up and two of my uncles built houses there.

I think I visited the Narsingdi estate in East Bengal only once. I remember visiting the local school, holding my eldest uncle's hand. The school was established by my grandfather, who named it after his father. That school is still there, in a much bigger form. It still carries the name of my great-grandfather, Kali Kumar Roy. I remember my eldest uncle's wife supervising the kitchen arrangements during our visit. As Aunt Anna was there with us, the *bawarchi* (chef) was trying his hand at Western cooking, and even baking cakes. There was much curiosity in the area's villages about the *memsahib* (white lady) in their midst, and a particular talking point was the bathroom and toilet specially built for her.

My father and his siblings also grew up in East Bengal, in a small town called Kishoregunj in the Mymensingh district (today the town is the centre of a full, separate district of Bangladesh). The family is from Banagram, a nearby village. I don't have any memories of my own about these places, but heard so much about them while growing up from Father, Mother and my paternal uncles that I almost feel I know them at first hand.

One such story is about *Durga Puja*—the autumnal worship of the Goddess Durga, the most important religious-cum-cultural festival of Bengal—in the ancestral property in Banagram. A buffalo would be slaughtered in a ritual offering to the goddess in the presence of a priest. After the animal sacrifice the men of the family would sing devotional hymns in unison.

The defining trait of my mother's family was clearly that they were 'doers', into social, political and entrepreneurial activities of various kinds. From all the stories I have heard about Kishoregunj, it seems my father's family were different—they were immersed in a world of literature, music and art. It's surprising that my paternal grandfather could foster such an environment of learning and culture in a remote East Bengal township. My father and his brothers all grew up fluent in English. Not entirely surprising, because they grew up staging home productions of Shakespeare's plays!

My paternal grandmother was a gifted singer. To encourage her, my grandfather had a harmonium brought from Calcutta. She was from a family sympathetic to the *Brahmo Samaj*, a reformist Hindu tendency that arose in Bengal in the nineteenth century. So she used to sing a lot of *brohmo sangeet* (songs of that sect) and, of course, songs of the new star in the firmament—Rabindranath Tagore. In the evenings she would sit with the harmonium and her children would gather around her and sing along. From that time music, especially Tagore's music, became an integral part of my father's family. It was unheard of in deeply provincial Kishoregunj that a housewife could also be a singer. Debabrata Biswas, later a maestro of *Rabindra sangeet* rendered in his inimitably original style, spent his childhood in Kishoregunj. He has written in his memoir about how my grandmother practised music and became the butt of ridicule in town as a result. She was undeterred. My mother told me that her mother-in-law would hum songs even while doing housework.

Shailaja Ranjan Majumdar, a familiar name in the world of Tagore music, was a close relative of my father's family. My father and uncles called him Shaila *bhatija* (nephew), as his grandmother was my grandfather, Upendra Narayan Chaudhuri's sister. He has written in his memoir that he was introduced to Tagore in the Kishoregunj house of my grandparents. Later in Calcutta he took Rabindra sangeet lessons from his 'Charu kaka', my father, Charu C. Chaudhuri. Not just Shakespeare, the children of the Chaudhuri household in Kishoregunj soon took to staging home productions of Tagore's plays. In a production of the play *Mukut* (Crown), my father played the crown prince and Uncle Nirad a rival prince. My mother told me that on another occasion the play *Bisarjan* (The Sacrifice) was being enacted. Uncle Manmatha was in the role of Raghupati the scheming priest. My youngest uncle Benode Chandra, who was playing the role of young Jai Singh, planted a (fake) sword in his own chest. Sitting in the audience was my grandmother, who fainted. On hearing of their mother's illness, Charu and Nirad set out for Kishoregunj from Calcutta. She died before they arrived. She regained consciousness just once, opened her eyes and said, 'I miss Charu and Niru.' Then she closed her eyes forever.

It was my maternal grandfather Lalit Roy who arranged the marriage of his daughter Chhaya-moyi (my mother) with Charu Chaudhuri. He had gone from Dhaka to Kishoregunj on some work. He told his family in Dhaka when he returned that he had met a very cultured family there whom he liked, so had mooted a matrimonial proposal. Chhaya was then in school, studying in the ninth standard. My grandfather Upendra Narayan, accompanied by his second son Nirad Chandra, came to Dhaka to check her out. My mother sang for them in Bengali while playing the *esraj*, a violin-like string instrument. Then she recited some Bengali poetry. The marriage was confirmed forthwith.

The wedding took place on the Narsingdi estate. To get there my father travelled by train and then boarded a *palki* or palanquin—a box-like thing with poles, carried on the shoulders of four sturdy men—for the last leg of the journey. A lively boy ran alongside the palki-bearers, all the while apprising my father about the bride, 'She is incredibly absent-minded, you know. She constantly loses keys.' There were several other odd attributes mentioned as well. Father used to say later that the boy's observations were completely on target. The excited boy was my mother's brother, Kiran, the favourite uncle of my childhood.

The night before the wedding Father bedded down in a room shared by a member of the bride's family who was suffering from high fever. In a delirious state, the man asked my father, 'Charu, do you know how many types of human beings there are?' 'No, I don't,' Father replied. 'There are two types—*pagol* [mad] and *chhagol* [goats, meaning fools],' came the reply.

There was another mishap during the wedding ceremony. Father objected when the officiating priest referred to Mother as *dasi* (servant) instead of *devi* (goddess). An argument broke out between the groom and the priest. The priest insisted that only Brahmin women were entitled to be called devi. Father refused to back down. To avert further embarrassment some of the guests persuaded the priest to use devi on the grounds that while not Brahmins these families were high caste (Kshatriyas, warriors in ancient times).

When the newly-weds reached Kishoregunj the bride was welcomed into her new home by a Rabindra sangeet chorus consisting of her five brothers-in-law and two sisters-in-law. From that point in 1920 Chhaya-moyi Roy became Chhaya Devi Chaudhurani. Because 'Devi Chaudhurani' was quite a mouthful Mother shortened her first name from 'Chhaya-moyi' to just 'Chhaya'.

Mother then moved to Calcutta—her husband and all his five brothers lived in the big city, working or studying. Father explained to her the crucial difference in East Bengali terminology between *bari* (home) and *basha* (house). Lodgings in Calcutta, however long term, were basha—a place to stay while working or studying. The home remained Kishoregunj.

But gradually the house became the home. My Kishoregunj grandmother passed away, and my grandfather chose a life of solitude and reflection in Kashi (Benares) after her death. My mother's two sisters-in-law were both married into East Bengal families but not in Kishoregunj. One moved to the town of Netrakona and the other to a place called Taljanga.

Home life in Calcutta was full of buzz and activity, because it wasn't just Mother and Father. Father's five brothers were constant visitors, as were many friends. The five brothers-in-law were quite a handful for Mother to deal with. All were talented in diverse fields and professions, and all were temperamental to varying degrees. And then there were Father's friends. One was the brilliant Bengali poet and literary critic Mohitlal Majumdar. Mother remembered dozing off while the dinner she had cooked went cold, as discussions about poetry and literature led by Mohitlal went on deep into the night.

Another friend and frequent visitor was the prolific novelist and short story writer Bibhuti Bhushan Bandyopadhyay, the leading chronicler of life and poverty in rural Bengal in the first half of the twentieth century. Bibhuti Bhushan became famous in Bengal in his lifetime, and after his death his work gained global recognition when his novel *Pather Panchali* (Song of the Road), published in 1929, was made into the path-breaking movie of the same name in 1955 by the director Satyajit Ray. Ray then made two further movies, comprising the 'Apu trilogy', based on the sequel to *Pather Panchali* (*Aparajito*, The Unvanquished) which Bandyopadhyay published in 1932. His relationship with Father was close. Once my parents decided to take a short holiday in Galudih, a resort-like place in today's Jharkhand state, neighbouring West Bengal. Bibhuti Bhushan, who knew the area well, wrote down detailed instructions about the local sights and 'must-do' things for them. Father carefully preserved that sheet of instructions afterwards.

Meanwhile my Shaejo kaka, Father's brother, Uncle Khirode, completed his studies at Calcutta's Medical College. He was keen to go abroad for further training but there was a problem. He had a police file because of alleged contacts with underground freedom fighters. This meant there was no possibility of getting a passport. One day he turned up and told my mother, '*Boudi* [older sister-in-law], please help me pack a suitcase fast. I'm leaving tomorrow.' He left the next day on a ship that sailed from Calcutta port; the ship needed a doctor on board and he had persuaded them to take him on. The ship took him to Boston in the United States. There he managed to acquire a passport and travelled to Europe. Over the next few years he studied paediatrics at the medical faculties of the universities of Tubingen in Germany and Vienna in Austria. He was penniless and had a tough existence. He would write to Mother about the hardship. Mother spoke to her father, my nationalist zamindar grandfather Lalit Roy, who arranged to send him money from time to time. Throughout her life Mother helped people in need, a trait she surely inherited from her father. Sometimes she overdid the altruism—my father's two youngest brothers would often tease her about her habit of jumping in to solve other people's problems.

Uncle Khirode arrived back from Vienna just in time to save my life. Aged one, I was seriously ill. The Europe-qualified specialist in infant and child medicine was aghast to find that his little niece had been subjected to all manner of quack treatment and was surviving on a compulsory diet of barley. The first thing he did was to feed me rice mixed with naturally nutritious foods with his own hands. I soon recovered. In that era in India, nobody had a clue how to properly treat sick infants and children. I was fortunate to be the first patient of Dr K.C. Chaudhuri, India's pioneer paediatrician.

DOVER LANE

'*Dada* [elder brother], I hear you are looking for a house in Ballygunge? What the hell are you thinking!' This was Uncle Nirad, making his opinion known as always. According to him, only social upstarts and the *nouveau riche* lived in Ballygunge, an area in south Calcutta. He himself lived in the *bonedi* (traditionally cultured) locality of Shyambazar in north Calcutta, the older part of the city, in an apartment building on Grey Street. But Father had fallen in love with a house in Ballygunge. The address: 7/2 Dover Lane. The second address of my life.

It was a low-slung, one-storeyed house, rather like a bungalow. What got Father hooked was that the property had a lot of outside space, and he badly wanted a garden. Even better, the neighbourhood was open and uncongested. There were just a few other houses on the street, all newly built two-storeyed structures with large gardens. Foxes roamed the area after dark. This was the second half of the 1930s. From around the time of Independence Ballygunge has been one of the most coveted addresses in Kolkata, and today the area is a mix of high-end apartment blocks and some old houses which remain from decades ago.

One of my first memories of Dover Lane relates to foxes. Uncle Nirad's wife, Aunt Amiya, had come over with her two very small sons to spend the day with us. Around dusk she was feeding the younger one milk from a *jhinuk*, a little container fashioned from a seashell. Suddenly she looked up and said to me, 'Did you hear? There are foxes calling!' I was thrilled—I had a fascination with foxes from Bengali nursery tales.

Thanks to Father's efforts our new house soon boasted a pretty garden. But our garden was dwarfed by the much larger lawns beyond the boundary wall. Those lawns belonged to a two-storeyed house with an impressive portico, facing out on Hindustan Road. The people who lived there were relatives of ours, Uncle Hem and Aunt Indu. Uncle Hem, Hemendra Kumar Das, was my father's maternal cousin. Aunt Indu came from a prominent zamindar family of the Mymensingh district in East Bengal. Her father Narendra Kishore Ray Chowdhury's older brother was Upendra Kishore Ray Chowdhury (1863–1915). Upendra Kishore, who was adopted into the family as a child, was a towering figure in the world of Bengal's culture—an accomplished writer, talented musician and artist, and successful publisher rolled into one. His son was the famous writer Sukumar Ray, and his grandson the renowned film director Satyajit Ray.

My mother visited Aunt Indu often, especially on festive and holy days, with me in tow. Aunt Indu was of a religious bent. I remember her *thakur ghar*, the worship room resembling a little temple found in traditional homes. I was especially fascinated by the miniature idol of *narugopal*, Lord Krishna as a child. I loved to watch Aunt Indu dress the blue-hued god with tiny shirts she made by cutting up her *benarasi* saris, the ornate sari worn by brides. A few other women frequented the house. One, whom I remember clearly, was a strikingly good-looking woman dressed in white, the widow's garb. She was the widow of Aunt Indu's older brother Dhirendra Kishore. Another woman in white was also a regular. This was Suprabha, the widow of Sukumar Ray, who died in 1923 aged only thirty-five.

I think there is a reason why I remember the Hindustan Road house so vividly. Our own Dover Lane house was usually rather quiet—just Father, Mother and me. But our neighbours' residence was always bustling. I loved observing all the activity, like a bird sitting on a branch. One day there was an air of excitement in their house. A lot of people, men and women, were waiting outside the closed door of a room. A few women including my mother were inside. After some time the door opened and Mother called out to me, '*Khuku* ['little girl', my nickname], come and see how beautiful it is.' I entered to find a new-born baby girl; my first glimpse of a new born.

Some of these memories are a bit fuzzy, like an Impressionist painting. But there are others I recall clearly. One day I was extremely excited. The older daughter of the Hindustan Road house was getting married. Father had promised me a sari to wear to the wedding. He and Mother had gone to New Market in central Calcutta to buy one. I was sitting by a window in the lap of Jhima, my fulltime nanny, eagerly awaiting their return. Jhima has been looking after me since our days in the house off Chowringhee and had moved to Ballygunge with us. At that time it was commonplace to call women servants as 'X's mother'. So when Jhima was hired my mother had asked her what her son's name was. It turned out she had no son, only a nephew whose name was Balai. So she was addressed by adults as *Balai-er Pishi* (Balai's paternal aunt). Since this was too much for me to handle, Mother told me to just call her 'Jhima'.

Soon my parents returned, carrying a number of packets. One of the packets revealed my first sari, in striking *firoza* blue with a silver *zari* border. On the wedding night I was traipsing around sari-clad. I noticed the huge number of saris the bride was getting as gifts and felt a little envious. During the ceremony I sat next to her. The holy fire burning in front of us made my eyes itch terribly. Then I began to doze off. Someone picked me up to take me away. I protested feebly, 'I don't want to go! I want to watch the wedding!'

The next day the bride left for her new home. A sombre mood in the house, the bride weeping profusely. A car was parked just outside the gate, and the new husband and wife walked towards it.

But the bride—whom I used to call *Didibhai* (older sister)—kept turning back from the gate in floods of tears and running back to her father. The sight upset me and I made a decision I confided to Mother, 'Ma, I'm not going to get married. I already have a sari, so I don't need to.'

The rhythm of life in our Dover Lane home gradually picked up. Neighbours dropped in frequently to introduce themselves and meet us. One day Father was busily gardening, dressed in khaki shorts and a white *genji* (undershirt). A lady who lived in the neighbourhood came to make our acquaintance. She saw him at work from behind and took him to be the family's *maali* (gardener). Despite the embarrassing introduction, this lady—I called her *mashima* (auntie, literally 'mother's sister')—became particularly close to us. She became great friends with Mother and taught her lots of new recipes for the kitchen. Mashima had several sons so I gained a few dadas (older brothers). The youngest son, Manikda, was especially active in *para* (neighbourhood) affairs. Mashima had one daughter, an exceptionally good-looking girl known by her nickname Monua. She became my Monuadi, an older sister.

The young men of our para got together and decided to form a neighbourhood club. They named it Hindustan Sangha ('*sangh*' or '*sangha*' means association). The club was inaugurated with much fanfare. The Ghosh family had a big house at one end of Dover Lane and the ceremony was held in their spacious downstairs living room. The Ghoshs' son, Alokda, was an exponent of the *behala*, a string instrument. He played, Manikda sang a song he had composed himself and I danced at the launch of the club. Monuadi dressed me in an orange georgette sari with a floral border. Holding a *rekabi*, a kind of designer plate, with a *pradip* (traditional flame) on it I managed a few 'dance' steps and hand gestures. It was the first public dance performance of my life.

In those days these sorts of neighbourhood clubs served various purposes. For some, the social and cultural activities were simply a cover for spreading the message of anti-colonial nationalism.

For others it was just the opposite, intended to divert youthful energy away from nationalism and into innocuous channels. Yet others were genuinely geared to cultural activity—dance, music, poetry—with perhaps a dollop of nationalism thrown in. I think our club belonged to this third type. The Hindustan Sangha definitely fostered a sense of community in our neighbourhood. I recall a *Poila Baisakh* (Bengali New Year) celebration one April. As was customary for children, I had received new clothes on the occasion—a light yellow frock with a collar and puffed sleeves in matching green. We walked in a *prabhat pheri* (early-morning procession) through the streets, singing in unison to welcome the New Year.

It was around this time that I first became acquainted with the works of a man called Rabindranath Tagore. He was such a tremendous presence in our house through his songs, poetry, plays and other creations that he seemed almost like a family member. Every evening, after returning from work Father would sit in our living room with his little organ and teach me to sing Tagore songs. I was nervous but he was very encouraging. Those were my first lessons in Rabindra sangeet.

On quiet afternoons Mother would sit me down and teach me the Bengali alphabet. I learned it the way generations of Bengali children have—by reciting simple phrases describing the ecosystem, populated by tigers in the forest, birds in trees and fish in rivers. Soon I graduated to writing down the lines of short poems—simple but beautiful—in a *khata* (notebook). Then Father taught me to recite these poems. My favourite poem can be rendered thus from Bengali: 'Yesterday the branch was empty… Today it's blossoming with flowers… Tell me o gardener… How did it happen?' It's still one of my favourite poems.

Our new surroundings helped dispel the loneliness I felt as an only child. The number of aunts and uncles grew as we got to know more and more families in the neighbourhood. Many families had little children around my age so my friends' circle expanded as well.

Our garden became a kids' playground. Father made a badminton court in a part of the garden. Both my parents were avid badminton players and other grown-ups in the neighbourhood would join them to play matches. We children were given small rackets to play amongst ourselves.

One day Monuadi appeared holding the hand of a little girl just my age: 'Look, I've brought you a new friend.' This was Minu, who had come to live in a house next to ours with her mother and brothers. Minu and I quickly became fast friends, and our families became close as well. A big difference between society then and now is how easily neighbours would become part of each other's lives. Minu had two older brothers, and I became their second little sister. It was a true sibling feeling.

One evening Father and Mother went to the cinema. I wanted to come but was disappointed when Father said this movie was meant for adults. The movie was *Vidyapati,* about the life of a poet-saint of that name who lived from 1352 to 1448. Born in Mithila (the northern part of today's Bihar state), Vidyapati's religious and romantic compositions have had a large impact and following over the centuries in Bihar, Bengal and Orissa. The movie starred Pahari Sanyal and Kanan Bala, also known as Kanan Devi—famous Bengali actors of that era of Indian cinema—as the male and female leads. Prithviraj Kapoor also played a major role. I know all this because my parents brought back the booklet about the movie the cinema gave to all patrons. I was especially impressed by the picture of Kanan Devi, a great beauty. The movie was a big hit of 1937, thanks mainly to its songs which became very popular. All the songs were printed in full in the booklet. The legendary Kidar Sharma composed the lyrics, and the screenplay was co-written by the famous Bengali poet Kazi Nazrul Islam.

To compensate me, Father promised to take me to the cinema to see a movie suitable for children. A few weeks later we watched *Robin Hood.* From that point, the do-gooder outlaw of medieval English folklore who helped the poor became my childhood hero.

The Sherwood Forest, his hideout, became part of my imagination and his associates—Little John, Will Scarlet, Friar Tuck and Maid Marian—became my favourite characters. I had to pay a price for abandoning my playmates the day we went to watch the movie. They retaliated by banning me from our games for two days. I remember standing by a flower-bed in our garden, crying, while the others played. The grown-ups had to intervene to get the ban lifted.

I used to be ill a lot as a child. Sometimes I felt like the boy-character Amal in Tagore's 1912 play *Dak Ghar* (The Post Office), who is confined to home due to illness. Mother and Father would bicker constantly over how I should be treated. If Mother wanted to call my paediatrician uncle, Dr K.C. Chaudhuri, Father would argue in favour of our family *kaviraj* (herbal healer), Bimalananda Tarkatirtha. And if Father wanted his brother to come, Mother would discover the merits of herbal medicine. So I alternated between traditional and modern treatments. Once Father's youngest sister had come to visit from Kishoregunj with her children. There was much eating and talking going on. I was in bed, unexcited by even the *jhuri* (basket) full of fresh mangoes that had arrived with the visitors. My aunt commented, 'This girl is so indifferent to everything!'

My birthday on 26 December provided another source of—or pretext for—arguments between my parents. If my mother wanted to buy a frock, my father insisted that I should be given a globe as a gift. I accompanied my parents to New Market, the famous covered market of central Calcutta established by the British in the nineteenth century where you can find practically anything you need or want even today in hundreds of shops. Eventually I was asked to resolve the disagreement by stating my preference but I was tongue-tied, intimidated by their argumentative habit. By this time I was wearing saris regularly. We would sometimes go to 'Glamour', a high-end clothing store in New Market which exists even today. Once there, Father and Mother would argue over whether a white or a pink sari should be bought for me. I learned to deal with this by endorsing my mother's preference for my birthdays and my father's for Durga Puja, the autumn festival of Bengal when the ten-handed Goddess Durga is worshipped and everyone, but especially children, wears new clothes. Later I realised that these were trivial disagreements. But as a child I would find them quite upsetting and respond by withdrawing into a shell.

The question of my schooling was also handled in a bizarre way. Father and his brother, my over-opinionated uncle Nirad C. Chaudhuri, decided that no school in Calcutta had a curriculum good enough for my education. Mother wanted me to be enrolled at Loreto House, the exclusive 'convent' or girls' school run by strict nuns where several daughters of relatives studied. She was impressed by how fluently these girls spoke English. Father objected on the grounds that the atmosphere there was too anglicised. So it was decided that Uncle Nirad's two sons, my first cousins, Dhruva and Kirti, and I would be home-schooled. This was a grave misjudgement on Father's part. I was already shy and diffident, a textbook case of only-child syndrome. Being deprived of the normal school experience compounded my isolation and made me even more inward-looking. I could not, and did not, learn how to make friends and socialise normally. I know that Indira Gandhi too suffered from being a lonely only child. Later she changed, at least in her public persona. But I remained an unconfident, withdrawn person well into my adult life. Much later I was compelled to come out of my shell and interact with the world around me. My isolated childhood meant that that was always a struggle.

Dhruva and Kirti were somewhat better off than me. They at least had each other, and soon another little boy was born to their parents. Moreover, once Uncle Nirad got a job and was too busy to teach them daily they had a private tutor hired to teach them at home. My existence was devoid of such human company, so books became my companions. Father, a compulsive and sophisticated bibliophile throughout his life, would buy lots of books for himself and for me. I soon read the ancient Indian epic tales, the Ramayana and the Mahabharata, in children's editions and would recite entire passages by heart to impressed relatives and neighbours. But my favourite book was *Robin Hood*, in Bengali translation. I would read it repeatedly. Sometimes I would not be mentally in Dover Lane but in the Sherwood Forest with the outlaw and his band of 'merry men'. Almost every day, after my neighbourhood pals returned from school, we would play by acting out the Robin Hood stories. I would invariably keep the Robin Hood role for myself. One playmate, Bablu, was rather fat and he would be Friar Tuck. Another, Tutu, was the tallest among us and he would be Little John.

Still, the Ramayana and the Mahabharata made me think about more serious things too. Does a Divine Being really exist, I wondered, when I watched Aunt Indu, our neighbour, lovingly bathe and dress her blue child-idol of Lord Krishna and put out meticulously arranged plates of food in front of the idol for the deity to consume. So I approached Father, 'Baba, does God really exist?' Father was relaxing in a chair in the yard behind our 7/2 Dover Lane house, enjoying the evening breeze while observing the stars in the sky, a lifelong habit of his. He replied, 'I don't believe in God. So I don't believe He exists. But over the ages many great men born in our country have said that He does exist. They are venerable people, who wouldn't lie or mislead for any reason. So once you grow up you will have to find the answer to this question yourself.'

After a few years in 7/2 Dover Lane we changed homes, but only next door to 7/1 Dover Lane. At our new address I was assigned a room as my study. From the window of my study I could see the leaf-filled branches of the big trees of the local Singhi Park swaying in the breeze and clear blue skies above. I would look and wonder: Is God somewhere there in the blue skies?

I found a resolution of sorts to my inner dilemmas when Father bought me illustrated books of *jataka* tales, stories and fables of the Buddha's lives prior to becoming the Buddha. In its pages, Prince Siddhartha searched for answers to why there was so much sadness and misery in human existence. Then he achieved *bodhi*, or enlightenment about the nature of life. Sorrow and joy are both intrinsic to being alive, the only path to liberation is through *nirvana*. There was a small brass statuette of the Buddha in a glass almirah in our living room. I took that out and placed it on a shelf in my study. Then I found a candle and a few other things and made a shrine. Unusually for a middle-class Bengali household there was no worship area (thakur ghar) anywhere in our home, not even an image or idol of Lakshmi, the goddess of wealth. This was probably because of Father's atheist beliefs, and the anti-orthodox spirit of the Brahmo Samaj—the nineteenth-century Hindu reform movement—inherited from my paternal grandmother was perhaps a factor as well. My private conversion to Buddhism was thus something of a departure. My Buddhist phase lasted for quite a while. It was during this phase that we went for the Durga Puja holidays to Rajgir, a place in Bihar closely associated with the Buddha's life. I loved Rajgir, a small town in a lush valley surrounded by hills, the capital of the ancient kingdom of Magadha (the town's name is derived from *raja-griha*, 'home of the royals'). By that time I already knew the story of Srimati from Tagore's 1926 dance-drama *Natir Puja* (The Dancing Girl's Devotion). Srimati was a palace maid and dancer who defied Ajatashatru, king of Magadha in the fifth century BC, and sacrificed her life for her Buddhist faith.

Speaking of Durga Puja holidays, my childhood memories are packed with such holidays in diverse and colourful locations of India. Affluent as well as comfortably off Bengali families of Calcutta would invariably go away for a month or so for the Puja holidays every autumn, and we were no exception. Many middle-class and lower middle-class Bengali families retain the habit to this day. It was quite an exercise. Trunks and suitcases would be packed with clothes and household necessities such as cooking utensils and crockery sets. 'Hold-alls'—bedding rolled up in an ingenious way—were also essential luggage. Then families would sally forth on their annual vacation. These were not nuclear-family outings—groups of relatives and close friends would plan their Puja vacation in advance and travel together.

The vacation in Galudih, Jharkhand I mentioned towards the end of the previous chapter I don't recall much of as I was very small. This was the place recommended to my parents by the writer Bibhuti Bhushan Bandyopadhyay. But there is one memory of that holiday I recall clearly. We had travelled somewhere in a fleet of bullock carts. Suddenly the two bullocks pulling one of the carts panicked and started running wildly. The cart tilted over to one side and cups, plates and containers of food spilled out. Years later I learned that we had gone to picnic in a forest atop a hill range. Everyone was having a good time, and footprints of wild elephants which had trampled on some of the vegetation added a note of excitement. In the late afternoon a Bengali family who lived in the area and were friends with Bibhutibabu came to join us, bringing high tea with them. That's when the mishap happened. The driver of their cart said that the bullocks had scented a tiger nearby. The picnic came to an abrupt end.

On another Puja vacation we went to Vindhyachal, a temple town in Uttar Pradesh's eastern region not far from Varanasi (Benares). We were accompanied by Father's close friend Phani Bhushan Chakraborty, a rising lawyer of Calcutta. Later, in independent India, he would become the first Indian chief justice of the Calcutta High Court, and briefly served as West Bengal's acting governor as well. On that trip I had a mishap that cut our holiday short. I was running around the courtyard of the town's famous temple dedicated to the Goddess Vindhyavasini, atop a hill overlooking the holy river Ganga, when I fell and suffered a deep gash in my leg. Soon I was down with high fever. Phani Uncle tried to cheer me up by composing a humorous rhyme in Bengali describing my predicament: *Pathe jete jete, pa-ta galo kete*—not really translatable into English. I think that was the first time I fell down and injured myself. This knack of accidentally

falling over and hurting myself would recur a number of times in my life.

On another Puja vacation we went to Deoghar, in present-day Jharkhand. The town is home to the Vaidyanath temple, a famous shrine dedicated to the deity Shiva. This time we were a big group. Our Dover Lane neighbours, Uncle Hem and Aunt Indu, were with us, along with their children. One day we were to visit the

ABOVE: *Justice Phanibhushan Chakraborty (1951)*

Vaidyanath temple to offer prayers. While tying my shoelaces Mother said to me, 'Make a wish at the *mandir* (temple) that you get a husband like Lord Shiva.' I nodded.

I remember the wet floor of the shrine, strewn with flower petals. I touched my forehead to the ground and made the wish. Later in life, I felt that God heard me and granted my wish.

The most memorable Puja vacation of my childhood was however in Darjeeling. It was autumn 1938, and I was seven. This 'hill resort' town, located at the northern tip of Bengal, is famed as the 'Queen of the Himalayas'. The area produces some of the world's finest teas. I had a thrilling experience soon after we arrived. This was seeing the Kanchenjunga massif at sunrise. Darjeeling has the best view of this massif. The sun's rays first illuminated the highest peak, then spread within minutes to bathe the whole snow-covered range in an ethereal glow. It was a glorious sight, simply unforgettable.

I loved the place we stayed in, called 'Retreat Cottage'. It had a circular drawing room with glass walls. The garden was blooming with flowers of many kinds and colours. Standing in that garden next to Father, I had my first glimpse of Kanchenjunga at daybreak. I returned to Darjeeling many times in the following years and decades. My Phul mama, my mother's brother, Kiran Roy, and his American wife, Aunt Anna, had a house called 'Balaclava' in Ghoom, a picturesque little town close to Darjeeling. After I got married, I had many occasions to visit the historic bungalow near Kurseong, another town in the Darjeeling district, which my father-in-law, Sarat Chandra Bose, had bought as a holiday home in the early 1920s. Netaji Subhas Chandra Bose spent quite some time in this bungalow, perched on a hill called 'Gidha Pahar' just outside Kurseong, in the 1930s. Later in life I've visited the Swiss Alps in Europe, as well as Kashmir several times. But the Darjeeling area has retained a special place in my heart ever since that first trip seventy-six years ago.

Phani kaka, the lawyer Phani Bhushan Chakraborty, was staying nearby at the Central Hotel. He hadn't come with us but was in Darjeeling for a work-related reason. The reason was a fascinating story in itself. Phani Uncle was representing one of the parties to the Bhawal case, one of the most bizarre and long-running court cases of late colonial India. Bhawal was one of the largest zamindari estates in East Bengal. The *kumar* (prince) of Bhawal, Ramendra Narayan Roy, had fallen ill and died during a trip to Darjeeling many years earlier and been cremated there. Some twelve years later a *sadhu* (ascetic monk) appeared and claimed that he was the prince of Bhawal. He claimed that those who had taken him to the Darjeeling crematorium thinking he was dead had left without cremating him due to inclement weather, and that after he regained consciousness he could not remember anything about himself. He was then taken in by a group of itinerant ascetics and wandered around India for years before gradually remembering who he really was. The prince's wife, the widowed *rani* (queen) of Bhawal, Bibhabati Devi, refused to accept this story and declared the man an imposter. She believed that the imposter was acting at the behest of some of her relatives. A lengthy court battle ensued; it went on from 1921 until the man's death in 1946. Phani Uncle was on the rani's legal team and had come to Darjeeling to investigate the origins of the matter.

I didn't understand any of the details then. I just knew that someone had disappeared and then come back. The Bhawal case was a celebrated and controversial topic in society, with strongly held opinions on both sides. Research monographs have been published on the case as recently as the last decade. My family too was divided on the matter. Father was sceptical of the sadhu's claims and was influenced by Phani Uncle's views as well. My maternal grandfather, Lalit Roy, himself an East Bengal zamindar, was on the side of the sadhu. They would argue bitterly over the issue. This was long before the advent of DNA technology so there was no scientific way of resolving the matter. Fingerprint technology was well-established but there were no fingerprints of the prince of Bhawal to test against the claimant's.

A Muslim judge was staying in the bungalow next to Retreat Cottage with his family. They would invite us to share *nashta* (breakfast) with them. During the daytime I would ride ponies in Darjeeling's famous Mall. Generations of children, particularly Bengali children, have done the same. The streets around the Mall, lined with shops, were so smart. The whole place had a strong English flavour, consistent with modern Darjeeling's origins as a Himalayan retreat for the colonialists and their families in the nineteenth century. I noticed immediately how friendly and kind the local people were. I made friends with several *kancha*s and *kanchi*s, local boys and girls of Nepali ethnicity. Since the 1980s the towns and tea estates of the Darjeeling hills have repeatedly resounded with the demand for a separate state of the Indian Union called Gorkhaland, a demand for recognition and autonomy raised by the descendants of those little boys and girls.

In the idyllic surroundings of Darjeeling, it was hard to know that Europe, and Asia, were on the brink of the bloodiest war in the history of humanity. The following summer I was sitting on the floor in our Dover Lane home, happily playing with my dolls. I was briefly distracted when I heard Father and other grown-ups excitedly exclaiming, 'England has declared war.' I couldn't understand what the fuss was about and soon went back to the dolls.

We spent the Puja vacation of 1939 in Puri, the popular beach resort of the state of Orissa and the site of the twelfth-century temple dedicated to another deity, Lord Jagannath. We rented a house on the beach. Here I saw the sea for the first time and was transfixed. Enormous waves appeared and cascaded down on the beach. I compared the sight to our light green hold-all, which when pulled out became a circular sleeping bag. It was a rather post-modern metaphor.

Uncle Nirad and his family were with us. Later my youngest paternal uncle, Benode C. Chaudhuri, also joined us. Uncle Nirad's two sons, Dhruva and Kirti, and I played on the sandy beach all day.

Robin Hood was passe. We played war games, between the Allies and the Axis Powers.

As Puja gifts, the two brothers had received air-guns, while I had been given a doll's house. It was a lovely two-storeyed doll's house, and included a drawing room, dining room and bedrooms. But it was of no use in our war game. So we were one air-gun short. We used a *khil*—a long piece of wood used to horizontally fasten a door—as our third weapon.

ABOVE: *Krishna enjoying a pony ride in Darjeeling aged six (late 1930s)*

Dhruva and I would represent the Allies while Kirti, the youngest among us, would represent the Axis. We would shoot him with the air-guns and tell him, 'You're dead.' One day Kirti rebelled. He refused to be killed. Instead he chased Dhruva along the beach and hit him with the khil. Dhruva started howling and the grown-ups came out of the house on hearing the commotion on the beach. Uncle Nirad announced that Kirti—in later life Professor Kirti Narayan (K.N.) Chaudhuri, a renowned historian who worked for most of his career in London's School of Oriental and African Studies (SOAS)—would stand in one corner of the dining room while the rest of us ate lunch. He would not be given any food for the rest of the day. We sat down to lunch. It was a delicious lunch, with different kinds of sea fish. I was barely able to eat, as Kirti stood in a corner watching us. My mother and Uncle Nirad's wife were aghast at the cruelty being meted out to a child but were too scared of Uncle Nirad to challenge him. At this point Father returned; he had gone out somewhere. He looked at the sombre company and said, 'What's happened?' Then he said, 'Kirti, you should not do this again, now come and sit down with us and have your lunch.' Uncle Nirad was overruled by his elder brother.

The vast majority of Indians revelled in Britain's reverses early in the war. This was entirely natural. After nearly two centuries of being 'the jewel in the crown' of Britain's colonial empire, Indians celebrated the humiliating defeats being suffered by their oppressors. One relative of ours would say 'Narayan, Narayan' whenever Hitler's name came up (Narayan is the name of the Supreme Being in Vedic Hinduism). People did not realise the demonic nature of Nazi Germany. Their consciousness was filled with the fervour generated by the Indian freedom struggle since the 1920s and with anger at the repression the British deployed against that struggle. In Bengal, thousands of young men had taken to armed struggle against colonial power since the first decade of the twentieth century. This revolutionary activity peaked during the first half of the 1930s. Over three decades hundreds of Bengal's finest youths had been executed by hanging and thousands sent to prison for protracted periods, often for life, or deported to such notorious detention centres as the Cellular Jail on the Andaman Islands in the Indian Ocean.

My uncle Nirad C. Chaudhuri was a glaring exception to the mood prevalent in India. A staunch loyalist of the Raj, he claimed to have used scientific methods to determine that Britain would win the war. He would get infuriated if anyone dared to disagree with him, and cut off any of his friends who did. He was completely intolerant, and at the same time would gain perverse pleasure from annoying others. At that time he used to live in a house on Chakraberia Road in south Calcutta's Bhowanipur neighbourhood, an area of educated middle-class Bengalis. He decorated his living room with a large portrait of Churchill, and was quite pleased when this attracted negative comment. My father was indulgent towards his younger brother. 'Niru is eccentric, you know,' he would say. The third of the brothers, my physician uncle, Khirode Chandra (K.C.) Chaudhuri, was less indulgent and would sometimes mock Uncle Nirad's views. Still, the family bonds were very strong and interpersonal relations within the family remained intact.

Uncle Nirad's stance had consequences for me. One day I came home early from playing with my friends in the Dover Lane neighbourhood, weeping profusely. Father and Mother were very concerned. At first I wouldn't say what had happened, then I blurted out, 'Tutu called me pro-British!' This was a huge insult. My playmate Tutu had heard Uncle Nirad broadcasting British war propaganda on All India Radio. Father started laughing. 'You should have told him,' he said, 'that his older brother is a pilot in the Royal Air Force. By the same logic, what does that make Tutu?' I didn't care about the logic. I was experiencing my first nationalist stirrings and was mortified by Tutu's taunt.

The daily rhythm of life on Dover Lane continued as usual. But the war engulfing much of the world intruded on our humdrum existence from time to time. One evening I was happily playing with my friends when one of our domestic helpers turned up, 'Father wants you to come home.' 'Five more minutes, please,' I replied. When I reached home I found Father sitting in our living room with an unusually sombre face. I wondered what had happened. 'Khuku, Paris has fallen,' he said. Father, although a lawyer by profession, was a connoisseur of art, literature and culture, East and West. He regarded Paris as a centre of world civilisation, and the news of its fall to the invading Germans made him deeply despondent.

Our para's Hindustan Sangha continued to stage cultural events. I was in the dance troupe. During one performance I committed a faux pas; I forgot to take off my spectacles before going onstage to dance to Tagore music. I did not realise it until my turn ended and the show's organisers gently rebuked me backstage.

There is a little story to how I got eyeglasses at the tender age of seven. Uncle Nirad used to live on Grey Street in the Shyambazar area of north Calcutta. Just opposite his apartment building was a building which had a tower with a circular clock. Just recently I was travelling through Shyambazar by car. I noticed the two buildings standing exactly as they were back then, in the late 1930s. The only difference was that the tower clock was not working.

Once when I was visiting them, Uncle Nirad's wife asked me to check what time it was on the tower clock. I went to the balcony of their flat to look, and could not make out the hands of the clock across the street. Within days I was taken to a dark chamber where my eyes were tested. As expected I had myopia, and already needed glasses with lenses of -3 and -3.5. The myopia of course got worse over the years. Just after my marriage—it must have been 1956—I was having a routine check-up with Dr Balai Mitra, a senior eye specialist of Calcutta. He told me jokingly, 'You are really myopic. Your children will be too.' As it turned out, all my three children needed glasses at an early age.

It was customary for neighbourhood clubs to stage plays during the Puja season every autumn. The Hindustan Sangha decided to put on a performance based on stories from *Raj Kahini* (The Saga of the Royals) by Abanindranath Tagore. Abanindranath Tagore (1871–1951), a nephew of Rabindranath Tagore, was primarily a painter, and an extremely gifted one. He devised a swadeshi model of art as an alternative to the Western schools of art taught to Indians under British rule by putting a modern, early twentieth-century twist on the Mughal and Rajput painting styles and traditions. He is regarded as the progenitor of the 'Bengal school' of art, the movement that provided the foundation for the development of Indian painting in the twentieth century. When not busy painting, Abanindranath loved to write books for children and *Raj Kahini*—a fictionalised narrative of Rajasthan royals in medieval times—is his best-known creation in this genre. I was given the role of a Rajput princess. Unfortunately, my otherwise open-minded and thoroughly modernist father refused to let me act in a production which included boys as well as girls. The formal reason given was that we were going away as usual for the Puja holidays. I was very disappointed. I still feel surprised that someone as enlightened as him stopped his ten-year-old daughter from acting in a play because of the presence of male actors of a similar age.

Although I had liked Puri very much, I had decided by this time that I preferred the mountains to the sea. I especially enjoyed our annual Puja holiday in Mussoorie, a popular resort town in the mountains of north India, in the present-day Indian state of Uttarakhand. On the journey to Mussoorie we visited Haridwar, a holy town where the river Ganga enters the plains of north India, and Rishikesh, another town known as the gateway to this part of the Himalayas.

The Ramakrishna Mission had a presence in Mussoorie, as it does in so many places across India, in some other countries of the subcontinent, and throughout Asia and the wider world. The Mission is inspired by the life and teachings of the nineteenth-century Bengali mystic Ramakrishna Paramahansa (1836–1886).

Ramakrishna's most famous disciple, the philosopher and social reformer Swami Vivekananda (1863–1902), founded the Ramakrishna Mission in 1897 to perpetuate Ramakrishna's ideal of service to humanity through welfare and development work for the poor, the needy and the distressed. Vivekananda's vision has been taken forward by generations of monks of the Ramakrishna order, and the Mission continues to be one of the most important global organisations of its type today. In Mussoorie we stayed in a bungalow. Swami Atulananda, an octogenarian American who headed the local Mission, lived in the bungalow just above ours. I would run up to his bungalow and he would give me locally grown apples. Because of his advanced age an Indian monk, Swami Anubhavananda, had been deputed to care for him. My mother would invite Anubhavananda over to eat with us. Father and he would engage in spirited discussions of religion and philosophy when he came over. Because of Father's atheist convictions the discussions would sometimes become heated. Father would ask him, 'What have you got by forsaking the worldly life?' The monk would get irritated. Mother would diplomatically intervene by announcing that the food was ready.

When we departed from Mussoorie my parents decided to trek down to the town of Dehradun (the capital of present-day Uttarakhand). It was a seven-mile trek along a rather sheer 'short cut' through the mountains. Just before we left we attended the annual sports competition of the residential school for boys in Mussoorie run by the Mission. It was fun, with tea and pastries served to the guests after the event got over. Then Anubhavananda joined us for part of the trek down to Dehradun. We stopped overnight in a village called Rajpur, where the Mission had an *ashram* or monastery. It was a serene environment; I still remember the flowers and the butterflies. The monks there were most hospitable and I recall the affection I received from them. For years afterward I was in touch through letters with my two friends in Mussoorie—the American monk Atulananda and the Indian monk Anubhavananda.

Shortly after this I had my first bereavement, at the age of nine. My maternal grandfather Lalit Roy fell seriously ill in Dhaka. He was brought to Calcutta. My maternal uncle Kiran Roy decided that his ailing father would be brought to our house on Dover Lane. Two of my other maternal uncles had houses in the Calcutta suburb of Jadavpur, close to the Bengal Lamp factory owned by the family. Uncle Kiran had a lovely flat on Theatre Road (now Shakespeare Sarani) in the poshest area of central Calcutta. But Uncle Kiran liked our modest, peaceful home on Dover Lane, especially during emergencies.

One such emergency had occurred a short time earlier. An older cousin brother of mine, on my mother's side, had a somewhat bohemian lifestyle. He was enjoying a rendezvous with his girlfriend at her house on Woodburn Road, a wealthy area in south Calcutta abutting the city centre, when they were disturbed. To escape detection he jumped from his girlfriend's second-floor bedroom and landed in the garden of 1 Woodburn Park, the adjoining house of my future father-in-law Sarat Chandra Bose (built in 1927). He broke a leg and needed a period of convalescence. It wasn't possible to take him to his own father's house; the father was furious with him. So Uncle Kiran arranged for him to recover at our house. I of course wasn't told the details of the incident but remember the man, his leg in plaster.

An ambulance stopped in front of our Dover Lane house. My study had been emptied and turned into a patient's room. *Dadu* (maternal grandfather) was brought out of the ambulance on a stretcher. Lying on the stretcher, Dadu put his hand on my head in a gesture of love and blessing. For a few days our house became a hive of activity, filled with doctors, nurses and relatives. Because meals were not being cooked as usual, a lady who lived down the street asked me to come and have lunch with her family. I ate with her children and she had just served the chutney to finish the meal—I loved chutneys—when the wife of one of my maternal uncles appeared. 'Come home, your father is calling you,' she said.

Father took my hand and led me to my study. He said, 'Dadu is going away, see him one last time.' I wasn't quite sure what 'going away' meant. I held tightly to Father's hand. I noticed a lot of people crying. I felt slightly guilty for not crying as well. It was 31 December 1939, five days after my ninth birthday on 26 December. We had had a joint birthday party for me and Uncle Kiran's wife, Aunt Anna, whose birthday was on Christmas Day. Our living room was still decorated with Chinese lanterns and multi-coloured paper chains tied from the ceiling fan—not in use in winter—to the four walls of the room. Just before my grandfather's body was taken out of the study to the living room, Uncle Benode, my youngest paternal uncle, switched on the fan. The fan whirred into life and the canopy of paper chains fell crumpled and severed to the floor.

WORLD WAR

After Dadu's death I travelled to Dhaka and the estate in Narsingdi with my mother and grandmother. For the first time I crossed the Padma river, the lifeline of Bangladesh, in a small ship. The Padma was so wide that we couldn't see one bank from the other, just water was visible. The ship was like a water-borne bus; it would stop at various points to set down and pick up passengers, then sail again. We got off at Narayangunj near Dhaka, and boarded a train. From the train compartment I could see the station's platform overflowing with people who had come to meet us; many were crying. Grandmother was asked to sit next to the window because they especially wanted to have a glimpse of her. I was a bit confused by the hubbub. Then Mother told me, 'They are your Dadu's *praja*s [subjects].'

Later I thought a lot about that experience. In the social structure of East Bengal until 1947 Hindu zamindars, owners of landed estates like my grandfather, were at the top. Their masses of prajas were overwhelmingly poor peasants from the region's Muslim majority, who provided for their families by working as serfs on the manorial lord's lands. It was a feudal arrangement and some zamindars and their underlings were notoriously cruel to the serf population. Not my grandfather, of course. He was a progressive man, an anti-colonial nationalist and social reformer who personally treated his serfs with dignity. But Mother also told me that when poor serfs could not pay the *khajna* (rent, in cash or kind) due to the estate, his officials would come down on them with a heavy hand. Resentment of Hindu landlords (and moneylenders) among the Muslim peasantry played a big role in the Pakistan movement gaining traction in Bengal during the 1940s, particularly in the Muslim-dominated east, leading to Bengal's Partition in 1947. Yet my personal memory from early 1940 is of Muslim serfs stricken with grief at the death of the man they clearly regarded not just as a provider but a father-figure. How complex these social relations were!

In Narsingdi I had a glimpse of life in rural East Bengal. My eldest maternal uncle, Nripendra Kumar Roy, took me to see the school established on the estate by my grandfather and named after my great-grandfather Kali Kumar Roy. We walked into a classroom. The teacher stood up immediately. It was an English class. My uncle put the textbook in my hand and asked me to read from it. Once I finished my uncle said to the teacher, 'Why can't our students read as well as this girl from Calcutta?' I felt very embarrassed; that's why I remember this incident. I know from friends in Bangladesh that the school is still there and thriving—it's no longer a primary school as it was then but a major high school of the area. It still carries my great-grandfather's name.

My eldest maternal uncle's wife was a gourmet cook. She had hired and tutored a bawarchi (Muslim chef) in the culinary arts. Across the yard was a smaller kitchen where my grandmother's meals were prepared separately—vegetarian food, as she was now a widow. Because Uncle Kiran and Aunt Anna were with us the big kitchen would bake cakes and biscuits in addition to the usual fare.

We returned to Dhaka and Narsingdi exactly a year later, over the New Year of 1940–1941, most likely for the ritual ceremonies on the first anniversary of Dadu's death. My tenth birthday on 26 December 1940 was celebrated on board the ship taking us across the Padma. The ship's cooks served up their famed chicken curry with rice, and produced a birthday cake as well.

On that trip my parents and I visited Kishoregunj in the Mymensingh district, the place my father's family are from. It was a nostalgic trip for Father to come back to where he was born and grew up with his five younger brothers and two younger sisters. We also visited his youngest sister, Sarojbala, who had married into the zamindar family of Taljanga, not too far from Kishoregunj. She was an exceptionally sweet person, and very close to my mother. Her father-in-law was Mahim Roy, the local zamindar; her husband, known by his nickname 'Gulu', was also a delightful person. I remember Father playing his organ and singing lustily in their living room. He was clearly re-living old times.

As I've mentioned, I was born in Dhaka, in my maternal grandfather's house in the Lakshmi Bazar neighbourhood of the city. My passport states my place of birth as 'Dacca, Undivided India'. But my only childhood memories of East Bengal are of these two trips at the age of nine and ten.

Our life in Calcutta was however like a slice of East Bengal transplanted to the west. My parents, maternal and paternal uncles and aunts would all converse in the *Bangal* dialect of East Bengal, common to Hindus and Muslims of the eastern region. This dialect is almost incomprehensible to people from West Bengal. There were subtle differences as well between the dialects of Dhaka and Mymensingh. Father would claim that the Mymensingh dialect was more lyrical, the Dhaka dialect rougher. This would enrage my mother. Mother had incredible culinary skills and she always cooked in the classic East Bengali style, with plentiful use of coriander and coconut. In 2006 I visited Dhaka with my younger son Sumantra and we were invited to lunch at the house of Sheikh Hasina, the current prime minister of Bangladesh and the elder daughter of Sheikh Mujib-ur Rahman, the founder of Bangladesh. Hasina had cooked for us herself. Eating her food, I was suddenly reminded of my mother's food.

On our departure on a winter night in January 1941, we were boarding a train at Kishoregunj station when I heard someone calling out to someone else in the Bangal dialect that the latter person had forgotten his '*tufla*' on the platform. Father explained to me that a 'tufla' meant a bundle—of clothing and possibly other things. I returned to Calcutta with a bundle of East Bengal memories.

Meanwhile the raging world war inched closer to Calcutta. Some young men in our neighbourhood joined the civil defence. They would walk around self-consciously with whistles dangling from their necks, like the traffic police. I became familiar with a new term: 'black-out'. All the houses were instructed to use dimmed lighting. Father covered the big ceiling lamp in our living room with an inverted brass bucket; the effect was of a fashionable decoration. Our glass doors were reinforced with strips of cloth cut in the shape of a cross to prevent easy breakage should bombs fall.

A new government office called the supply department was set up for the war effort and provided jobs to many. The war also spawned a new class of private entrepreneurs. A man we knew went from rags to riches by supplying caps for military use.

An event with historic consequences happened in Calcutta around that time. At about 1.30 am on 17 January 1941 Subhas Chandra Bose secretly escaped from the Bose family's house on Calcutta's Elgin Road, today Lala Lajpat Rai Sarani. The Elgin Road house, known as Netaji Bhawan since Independence, was built by Netaji's father, Janakinath Bose, in 1909 on the family's arrival in Calcutta after nearly twenty-five years in the city of Cuttack in Orissa, where Janakinath practised law and Netaji was born. Netaji escaped in the dead of night from the Elgin Road residence in a German-built Wanderer car driven by his twenty-year-old nephew—my future husband, Sisir Kumar Bose. Sisir was then a student at Calcutta's Medical College. When the news of Bose's disappearance became public some ten days later it caused quite a stir. I don't remember my parents or other adults discussing that, though. I do have a memory from some months or perhaps a year or so later. Father and Mother had shut all the doors and windows of our house and were listening to someone called 'Subhasbabu' broadcasting on the radio—from Berlin, I was told. Not everyone on Dover Lane had a radio in their house. Occasionally neighbours would come over to listen to the broadcasts—all very surreptitiously, as tuning in to Bose's broadcasts was a grave offence.

After my marriage to Sisir in December 1955 I lived for nearly two decades in 1 Woodburn Park, the beautiful and spacious house built on Woodburn Road—an elegant street just off Elgin Road—by my father-in-law, Sarat Chandra Bose, in 1927. Woodburn Road is now Bivabati Bose Sarani, named in honour of my mother-in-law. I used to visit the Woodburn Park house, one of Calcutta's best-known addresses at the time, as a child. This was because Uncle Nirad was working as secretary to Sarat Chandra Bose, a leading barrister and prominent nationalist leader who was his younger brother Subhas's lifelong confidant and supporter. Once Father and I had dropped by there when we saw a distinguished-looking gentleman getting into a car in the house's portico. He paused when he saw Father and they had a brief conversation. I remember Father being unusually excited—Sarat Bose was a big name both in the legal profession and in nationalist politics.

My childhood memories of 1 Woodburn Park are of flowers, birds and dogs. At that time Uncle Nirad used to live on Chakraberia Road in south Calcutta, quite close to Elgin Road and Woodburn Road. His manservant Dhonu sometimes took me, Dhruva and Kirti over to 1 Woodburn Park in the late afternoons. The house's garden was a riot of colour, with lots of different types of flowers in bloom. Birds chirped on its trees. And there was a dog, a Great Dane called Flash. Some early evenings Uncle Nirad would appear in our Dover Lane house with Flash on a leash, having walked over from 1 Woodburn Park.

The house on Chakraberia Road where Uncle Nirad lived as a tenant was a typically labyrinthine old Calcutta house, ideal for children's games. We would play hide-and-seek in the passageways on the ground floor, and a crocodile game in the inner courtyard. One morning I had a rather different experience. Father and I had dropped by there to see Uncle Nirad. We found the ground floor a mess, strewn with books, papers and various personal effects taken from the ransacked room of another tenant. I knew that tenant, a young man I addressed as kaka. He had been taken away by the police during the night. I did not know that the genial youth I knew as Tridib kaka was a freedom fighter—Tridib Chaudhuri, a founder of the Revolutionary Socialist Party (RSP) formed in 1940 by members of the Anushilan Samiti, a famous revolutionary society of colonial Bengal. In independent India Tridib kaka was elected no less than seven consecutive times to the Lok Sabha (House of the People), the directly elected chamber of India's Parliament, starting with the first Lok Sabha elected in 1952. He would stand from his home district Murshidabad about 200 km north of Calcutta. At the time of his death in 1997, a year after I was elected to the Lok Sabha for the first time, he was a member of the Rajya Sabha, Parliament's indirectly elected upper chamber.

Much later in life I visited that Chakraberia Road house many times. The house was owned by the family into which my eldest sister-in-law—Mira, Sarat Bose's oldest daughter—had married. Whenever I visited them there after my marriage I would recall those memories from the early 1940s.

Amid the clouds of war, we had a happy family occasion. One of my younger paternal uncles, Manmatha Chandra, got married to Padmalaya, a woman from a cultured family and the niece of a well-known Calcutta barrister. Our Dover Lane house became a hive of activity for the wedding. A lovely *shamiana*—a canopy-like structure of brightly patterned cloth—was erected on the next-door lawn of Aunt Indu and Uncle Hem for the wedding reception. Father decided that the reception would consist of high tea rather than the usual dinner. Small round tables with chairs were set up in the shamiana and high tea was served to the guests. Although it was February and the weather was still cool, an ice-cream counter was set up on one side of the garden. Aunt Anna wowed the guests by turning up in a traditional *dhakai* sari, handmade by weavers in Dhaka. This sort of unconventional wedding reception was unheard of in Bengali society, but Father's idea of doing something different proved to be a big hit.

Father had also decreed that there would be no ululating nor blowing of conch shells during the wedding rituals. The reason: he had recently read in Western anthropology texts that these noises used to be made in oriental societies to ward off evil spirits. The ban sent the women of the family into a tizzy. They could not imagine welcoming a new bride without ululating and blowing on conch shells. Aunt Neelima, my doctor uncle Khirode's wife, was sent to negotiate with Father on their behalf. She extracted a concession from him—no ululating, but conch shells could be sounded.

After the wedding, the entire Chaudhuri family assembled for a group photograph. Usually family portraits and photographs would be taken by Parimal Goswami, a well-known photographer of Calcutta who was also an author. Over the years he had become

BELOW: *The Chaudhuris (1942)*

a family friend and I called him Parimal kaka. On this occasion, for the first time, the photograph was clicked by William Pereira, a Sri Lankan who had settled in Calcutta. Seven decades later, the Pereira family's photography and photo-processing business is still going strong in a residential neighbourhood in south Calcutta, led by the Sri Lankan immigrant's son and grandson. The February 1942 family photograph is a precious one in the Chaudhuri family's albums.

Around this time a new address entered my life. Father bought a little house in a peaceful, scenic place called Mihijam on the Bengal–Bihar border, in the Santhal Parganas district (today Mihijam is in Jharkhand, just beyond the West Bengal border). The Santhals are an *adivasi* (indigenous) community who live in some rural parts of eastern India; their largest concentrations are in the present-day states of West Bengal and Jharkhand (Jharkhand was formed as a separate state of the Indian Union from southern Bihar in 2000). It was a one-storeyed bungalow set in a sizable plot of land. By the boundary wall there was a tree blooming with crimson flowers. The property had a well with a mature *ata* (sugar apple or custard apple) tree next to it. I had just received my first camera—a Kodak box camera. I clicked a photograph of my parents having tea under the tree and proudly named it 'Under the Custard Apple Tree'. Father named the house 'Benubon' after a Buddhist *vihara* (monastery) in the present-day state of Tripura in the far north-east of India.

ABOVE: *Krishna's parents having tea under the custard apple tree in the garden of their vacation home in Mihijam, Santhal Parganas (early 1940s)*

Father could now indulge his love of gardening as never before. Mihijam was famous for its roses. He laid flower beds with different varieties of roses. A bougainvillea tree added another, startling dash of colour. After we acquired 'Benubon' our holidays in various mountain and sea resorts became much less frequent. We would instead go to our own retreat in Mihijam at every opportunity. The lawyer Phani Bhushan Chakraborty, Father's close friend and my Phani Uncle, who often joined us on holiday trips, was one of the first visitors to our new holiday home. The house needed a caretaker and we were lucky to find Gokul, a hardworking and trustworthy local man.

Mihijam had a beautiful natural setting. It was overlooked by a hill range. At the foot of the range was a Santhal village called 'Mahulbona'. The Ajoy river was a short distance away. The bank of the Ajoy was a perfect spot for picnics. Once a week there would be a *haat*, a local market. I was especially attracted by the glass bangles on sale there. When the haat got over the Santhal girls would walk back to their village singing traditional songs in chorus.

ABOVE: *Mahulbona, the Santhal village in Mihijam (mid 1940s)*

Our Mihijam house held special meaning for all members of the Chaudhuri family. My father and uncles had left home and hearth behind in East Bengal to migrate to Calcutta, for higher education or employment or both. None of them had a really permanent address in western Bengal. We did not own our Dover Lane homes—7/2 and 7/1—we were simply long-term tenants. When Father bought the bungalow on the Bengal–Bihar border, all the Chaudhuris in migratory exile from their East Bengal homeland found an address to call their own. It became a favourite destination for the extended family.

A number of Calcutta families, more affluent than ours, already had holiday homes in Mihijam. These homes had poetic names: 'Dharma-Dham' (Abode of Faith), 'Shanti-Kunja' (Abode of Peace), and so on. Once a group of young men came from Calcutta for a vacation and decided to annoy the residents. They used pieces of charcoal to write *Adharma-Dham* (Abode of Sin) and *Ashanti-Kunja* (Abode of Unruliness) on the walls of these houses. Our house escaped their attention initially, until we woke up one morning to find '*Dhenubon*', a parody of 'Benubon', scrawled on our wall. The pranksters provided a nice touch of comedy to the sleepy place.

Mihijam is a wonderful part of my childhood memories. I still remember the lovely sight of the full moon at night, high above the silhouetted forests of *saal* and eucalyptus trees.

Whilst we were preoccupied with our family wedding and the excitement of our new holiday home in the Santhal Parganas, events of historic significance to India were taking place as World War II deepened and spread. In February 1942 Singapore, the fortress of British power in Asia, fell to the Japanese. Some 45,000 Indians, junior officers and soldiers, surrendered to the Japanese as part of the British capitulation. Many of these men would form the core of the Indian National Army (INA), 'Azad Hind Fauj' in Hindustani, the force of freedom fighters led from 1943 to 1945 by Netaji Subhas Chandra Bose. Three decades later I sat in 1 Woodburn Park listening to Fujiwara Iwaichi (1908–1986), a Japanese military intelligence officer who was present at the

RIGHT: *Benubon, Mihijam (mid 1940s)*

Singapore surrender, describe the dramatic scenes that unfolded in Singapore's Farrer Park that day in 1942. Fujiwara, who had been tasked by his superiors with building up the anti-British liberation movements in Southeast Asia, told the surprised Indian soldiers that if they wished they could fight for India's freedom. Most of the Indian POWs responded enthusiastically by throwing their caps in the air. The mercenaries of colonial empire were transformed into fighters for national independence, giving rise to a movement that swept through the three million-strong Indian diaspora in Southeast Asia and peaked after Netaji arrived in Singapore in mid-1943. Colonel Fujiwara, a ramrod-stiff military man in the best *samurai* tradition, continued to work with Netaji and in the process made an invaluable contribution to India's freedom from two centuries of colonial subjugation. He retired in the mid-1960s as a lieutenant-general in Japan's self-defence forces, set up under American tutelage after World War II. When he died in 1986 a telegram from Japan reached our home in 90 Sarat Bose Road, Calcutta: 'Fujiwara returned to Hindustan forever.'

In 1939, as World War II approached, Subhas Bose had urged his fellow Congress leaders, above all Mahatma Gandhi, to turn Britain's crisis into India's opportunity by launching an all-out struggle against the Raj. In 1939 and 1940 Gandhi and most of the Congress leadership dithered. But in 1942 Gandhi changed his mind. He dismissed vague promises of self-government after the war made by Sir Stafford Cripps, an emissary of the Churchill government, as 'a post-dated cheque on a crashing bank'. Subhas, in his radio broadcasts, had entreated Gandhi to reject the Cripps mission. Then on 9 August 1942 Gandhi called on the British Raj to 'quit India'. This was the ultimatum backed by a mass agitation Bose had called for in 1939 and 1940, prior to his departure from India.

Aged eleven, I started reading newspapers around this time. We would get *The Statesman* at home; this Calcutta paper, while well-edited, was no more than a mouthpiece of the Raj and the interests of British people living in India. The Bengali daily *Anandabazar*

Patrika provided the popular, nationalist viewpoint. One morning I was reading the papers when I saw Father putting on a tie as he got ready to go to work. I said, 'Baba, it says in the newspaper that crowds in the streets are forcing those wearing ties to take them off and then burning them in bonfires.' Father replied, 'No problem, my tie is made of pure *khadi*!' Indeed it was of khadi (or *khaddar*), the hand-spun cotton-based fabric long promoted by Gandhi and favoured by nationalists. It was de rigueur for members of the Indian National Congress to wear khadi clothes. Father's khadi tie was cream in colour and decorated with small blue stars. He went off and returned sheepishly a short while later, sans tie.

The British government launched a massive crackdown on the Congress as soon as the 'Quit India' movement was announced. Almost all senior Congress leaders were arrested and spent the duration of the war in prison. The British sought to decapitate the movement at birth but were not entirely successful. Mass uprisings broke out in different parts of the country. Anything representing the government's authority, beginning with police stations and administrative buildings, were targeted across India by mobs. In some places the movement took the form of organised insurgency and 'liberated zones' were proclaimed. One such place was the Medinipur (then Midnapore) district in Bengal, where revolutionaries drove out all traces of the government and declared a *jatiya sarkar* (national government). British forces recaptured the area with much difficulty and after resorting to atrocities on the population. The women of Medinipur were at the forefront of the rebellion. Many confronted the police and military with *bonti*s, a sharp tool used for cutting and chopping in the kitchen. A septuagenarian widow, Matangini Hazra, was shot dead while leading a march. She was one of countless martyrs—men, women, even children—of the Quit India campaign. Within a couple of months the British wore down the movement with relentless repression, although a few rebel bastions like the Tamluk area of Medinipur held out for significantly longer.

The waves of revolt reached even sleepy Mihijam! That autumn, when we arrived in Mihijam for our usual sojourn during the Durga Puja vacation our caretaker, Gokul, told us about it. A group of young men uprooted a section of the train tracks close to Mihijam station (sabotage was a widespread tactic of the Quit India campaigners). Chased by the police, they came running towards our house, jumped the boundary wall, scaled another inner wall and hid in our courtyard. They managed to evade the police on that occasion.

A few key organisers of the revolt were still underground, evading arrest. Household names like Jaya Prakash (J.P.) Narayan and Aruna Asaf Ali were among them. One day my Phul mama came over to our house on Dover Lane and had a long conversation with Father. Aruna Asaf Ali needed to move shelters and Uncle Kiran wanted to put her up in our house for a bit. She was a Bengali, born Aruna Ganguly. I was thrilled at the prospect. Unfortunately Father chickened out, or he put the safety of his family first. He told Uncle Kiran that pro-British families lived on the street so it would be too risky.

A year before the Quit India movement, a defection had taken place from the ranks of Indian political activists to the side of the British. Subhas Bose's supporters were mostly leftists. This was even more so after his break with Gandhi and the socially and ideologically conservative wing of the Congress in 1939. Most of Bose's left-wing supporters stayed steadfast in their pursuit of India's freedom and many were active in the Quit India movement. There was however one small faction who became renegades to the cause of national independence. This was the Communist Party of India (CPI), which radically changed its outlook and approach after Nazi Germany attacked the Soviet Union in June 1941. The CPI collaborated with the British government against Indian freedom fighters for the rest of the war and many freedom fighters were caught and jailed, or even killed, as a result. The CPI actively opposed the Quit India movement and did whatever it could to help the British put down the uprisings. The CPI did a lot of damage to the independence struggle and represented a particular danger to left-wing freedom fighters with whom the party had had prior connections. J.P. Narayan and Aruna Asaf Ali, on the run from British police and intelligence, were both members of the socialist wing of the Congress party.

Many years later I realised just how much harm the Indian communists had done to India's freedom struggle during World War II. After my marriage to Sisir Bose, Sarat Bose's son and Netaji's nephew, in December 1955 I lived at 1 Woodburn Park until we moved out from there in 1974. My husband, a paediatrician by profession, was also an ex-freedom fighter who had endured great personal suffering—imprisonment and torture—as a youth during World War II. I realised soon after we got married that he was obsessed with documenting every aspect of Netaji's life and work, especially the climactic period of 1941 to 1945. He would get hold of people who had worked closely with Netaji and invite them over to Woodburn Park to stay with us while he recorded their testimonies. I soon got used to this sort of guest in our home.

One day in the early 1960s Sisir told me, 'We have someone coming to stay who played a very important role in helping Netaji at a crucial time. But later he betrayed us and because of his treachery many freedom fighters, me included, were caught by the British. But I want to record his experiences of working with Netaji, so he will be our guest for a few days.'

The man was Bhagat Ram Talwar, who played an important role in Netaji's escape from India in early 1941. After Sisir drove his uncle on the first leg of the escape from Calcutta to the Gomoh railway junction in Bihar (now Netaji Subhas Chandra Bose Gomoh Junction in Jharkhand), Netaji took a train, the Kalka Mail, from there to Peshawar. Bhagat Ram, a leftist activist in the (then) Frontier Province, was Netaji's companion and guide in the difficult journey from Peshawar to Kabul. After reaching Kabul Netaji was stuck in the Afghan capital for forty days and Bhagat Ram, who used the pseudonym Rahmat Khan, was with him. He thus had invaluable personal testimony and Sisir was determined to get it from him.

Bhagat Ram was a charming guest. He played with our little son and heartily enjoyed Bengali fish-and-rice lunches. The rest of the time he would sit and recount his time with Netaji in early 1941 and Sisir would take it down on an Olivetti typewriter. What passed unmentioned was that Bhagat Ram was a communist whose allegiance changed after mid-1941. In the early 1980s a Czech-American scholar, Milan Hauner, published a book called *India in Axis Strategy* based on much archival research. The book showed beyond any doubt that Bhagat Ram had worked simultaneously as an agent of the British, the Germans, the Soviets and the Indian freedom movement after mid-1941. Netaji apparently never suspected him and maintained contact with him. He was thus an invaluable asset for the British. Among other things Bhagat Ram helped the British crack the mystery of Netaji's escape from India and those who had played key roles in the escape—Bose loyalists Mian Akbar Shah and Abad Khan in the Frontier Province, Sisir in Calcutta—all fell into the British dragnet one after another as a result. Bhagat Ram was never arrested. The amazing thing is that Bhagat Ram came from a *shaheed* (martyr) family—an older brother of his, a freedom fighter, had been hanged some years earlier by the British.

But I learned about all this drama much later. Meanwhile as 1942 yielded to 1943, the war engulfing Southeast Asia came closer and closer to Calcutta. After the Japanese overran Burma (Myanmar) a lot of Bengali families settled in Burma for employment or business fled to India. Several families we knew came from Rangoon (Yangon) to Calcutta as war refugees. The big question was what the Japanese would do next. A fear psychosis spread in Calcutta, especially among bourgeois Bengali families. I learned a new English word: 'evacuate'. Scared to death by the prospect of Japanese air attacks on Calcutta, more and more such families started to 'evacuate' the city. Around this time Father got me admitted to the Gokhale Memorial School for Girls, a reputed school of Calcutta. I think he had belatedly realised that he had made a mistake, under Uncle Nirad's influence, in not sending me to school and that I was being deprived of a fully normal childhood as a result. I was happy but as fate would have it a couple of months later the school evacuated to either Ranchi or Hazaribagh (I forget which), towns in present-day Jharkhand.

To evacuate or not to evacuate? My parents could not make up their mind for quite some time. By this time Uncle Nirad had moved to Delhi to work for All India Radio there. My parents and I visited Delhi after he moved there, my first trip to the capital. We rode a *tonga*—horse-drawn carriage, the taxis of Delhi at that time—around the city. I was very impressed by the centre of New Delhi, a vast space dotted with stately buildings—North Block, South Block, Parliament House (then the central legislative assembly building), Rashtrapati Bhavan (then the viceroy's palace). The imposing buildings of course looked even bigger to a child. During my years in Parliament (1996–2004) I would often remember that first visit—a small girl sitting in a tonga amid the architecture of colonial power.

ABOVE: *The families of Charu C. and Nirad C. Chaudhuri, Delhi (late 1940s)*

Uncle Nirad opined from Delhi that it was unnecessary to leave Calcutta. Father and Uncle Khirode felt differently. Eventually it was decided that the women and children would go to the house in Mihijam. Mother, Uncle Khirode's wife Aunt Neelima and I would travel there from Calcutta. Uncle Manmatha, recently married, was an engineer at the Tata family's industrial complex in Jamshedpur, in present-day Jharkhand. There were rumours that the steel plant there might attract a Japanese air strike, so his wife, Padmalaya, would also join us in Mihijam. Because the women could not be all alone in a village on the Bengal–Bihar border, Father's youngest brother, my Uncle Benode, took leave from his job in Calcutta to stay with us in Mihijam. Uncle Benode was a somewhat hot-tempered but deeply lovable person, with a heart of gold. Because of his eccentric nature my children called him *pagla* dadu (crazy grandpa). At that time he worked in the publications division, based in Calcutta, of Visva-Bharati, the university established by Rabindranath Tagore in Santiniketan ('Abode of Peace') in Bengal's Birbhum district, north-west of Calcutta. He soon noticed I loved books and would regularly give me books whose publication he had supervised as gifts. I loved those beautifully produced books—they had yellow covers with the title and author's name printed in red on the yellow background. Some were books of Tagore's poetry. Once he gave me a book in which Tagore recounted his travels in Japan and Iran. That was my favourite.

One morning in April 1943 we evacuated from Calcutta. Uncle Khirode, my doctor kaka, drove us to Mihijam. I had passed a nearly sleepless night. The previous evening Mother and I had arrived in Uncle Khirode's house on Creek Row in central Calcutta with our luggage. My luggage included a cage with two snow-white rabbits, my pets. Uncle Khirode declared that he wouldn't allow the rabbits in his car. I was devastated at the thought of being separated from them. In the morning, however, he took the cage and put it in front of my legs where I sat on the rear seat.

We drove along the Grand Trunk Road, the famous Calcutta-Delhi connector. Soon we left the city behind and there were paddy fields on both sides, interspersed with ponds. We stopped briefly by one such pond in a shady grove of tall palm trees. The rabbits were let out and ate some grass. In the bustling town of Bardhaman (then Burdwan) a late breakfast at an acquaintance's house awaited us. Then we pressed on to Asansol, the last major town in Bengal before Bihar. There we had lunch. By 3 pm we had arrived in Mihijam. Uncle Khirode drove back to Calcutta the same day. Our strange exile as wartime evacuees began.

Mihijam was buzzing with life in a way I had not seen before, even during the Puja vacation the previous autumn. Frightened by the spectre of the Japanese, dozens of 'evacuee' families from Calcutta had retreated to their holiday homes. Some of these families were of a conservative mentality. They were appalled that Mother played badminton every day with her brother-in-law—Uncle Benode—on a makeshift court in a corner of our garden.

Soon after our arrival Tagore's birthday—the twenty-fifth day of the Bengali month of *Baisakh*—came up at the end of the first week of May. Tagore had died less than two years earlier in August 1941, so sentimentality was at its peak. Tagore's death was felt as a personal loss by vast numbers of Bengali families. I remember that the news of his passing arrived while we were attending a family wedding. I recall breaking into tears at the wedding venue. I was a child of ten and far from able to appreciate the magnitude of Tagore's genius, but even at that age I felt a sense of colossal loss.

The evacuee families, conservative and liberal, gathered together to observe the birth anniversary. Aunt Padmalaya was the star of the event; she sang very well and excelled at Rabindra sangeet. An enraptured man in the audience announced that he would give her a medal.

Father was in touch from Calcutta. He would send me English lessons by post. I would write the answers and post back. That was about the extent of my studies. The atmosphere in Mihijam was too fun and laid-back for serious studying. There was now a chicken-coop in the courtyard of our house, with a rooster and a hen. I named them Rumki and Jhumki. My days were filled with chasing them around the courtyard. When the hen produced eggs I would write down the date on the eggs. Then I would wait impatiently for the eggs to hatch.

BELOW: *Krishna in the garden of the vacation home in Mihijam, Santhal Parganas (mid 1940s)*

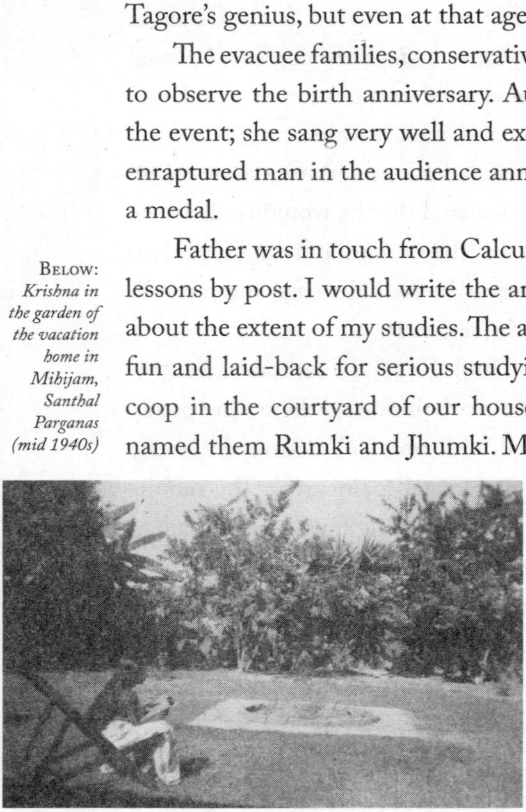

I didn't lack for human company either. My friend Minu from Dover Lane had also 'evacuated' with her mother to a house close to the Mihijam railway station. Uncle Manmatha would turn up periodically from Jamshedpur. He was also musically inclined and the open verandah in front of our house became a venue for evening soirees.

ABOVE: *Krishna at the family's holiday home in Mihijam, Santhal Parganas (mid 1940s)*

There was just one problem. The weather became unbearably hot as summer set in. There was of course no electricity, so there were no electric fans as in Calcutta. The evenings were dimly lit with oil-fired lanterns, which made for a surreal atmosphere. The only way to pass the stiflingly hot nights was to sleep out in the open. We would bed down in the garden every night. The eucalyptus trees would rustle in a gentle breeze. All was fine until an *aandhi*—a dust storm—struck one night. We grabbed our bedding and raced inside the house for shelter.

It became so hot that my mother and aunts could no longer keep on the heavy gold bangles they had all worn on their forearms since getting married. They dispensed with the heat-conducting jewellery. Then one day the sky turned overcast with monsoon clouds. First large drops of rain fell, then there was a torrential downpour. All of us, adults and children, came out into the garden and got soaked. It was like an impromptu festival.

An entire sub-genre of Tagore songs is inspired by the rains in Bengal. So a cultural show was organised to welcome the rainy season. Minu's older sister became our dance instructor. Dressed in simple printed saris with leaf motifs, we children danced in unison to Tagore's monsoon songs. I did a solo dance as well, and made more of an impression than I realised at the time. Thirty-nine years later in April–May 1982, I was undertaking a door-to-door campaign in south Calcutta—accompanied by the young and then unknown Congress activist Mamata Banerjee—for my husband, Sisir, who was standing for election as a Congress candidate to the West Bengal legislative assembly (he won). In a house in the middle-class Bhowanipur neighbourhood a man told me, 'I saw you dance ages ago, in Mihijam during World War II. I even remember the song you danced to.'

As the rainy season progressed, more and more of the evacuees in Mihijam started getting restive. They were big-city urbanites and the rural sojourn became suffocating after a while. Dacoit raids during rain-soaked nights on a couple of houses didn't help. The local dacoits seemed to be a more immediate menace than the Japanese, who had not yet got around to bombing Calcutta. Mother missed Father and went to visit him in Calcutta for a fortnight. That was the first time, aged twelve, that I was separated from both my parents. Mother would write to me every day. 'Don't bathe immediately after playing badminton,' one of her letters—all written in Bengali—read. 'Rest for a little while and once the sweat has gone take a light bath. Then put the powder on yourself.' There was news from Calcutta too in the letters. Mother and Father went to the cinema to watch a movie called '*Jhoola*', a classic of early Bollywood starring Leela Chitnis and Ashok Kumar. Its music, by Saraswati Devi, was a huge hit and in 1943–1944 soldiers of Netaji's Indian National Army set the lyrics of a number of INA songs to its tunes. Saraswati Devi was the assumed name of Khorshed Minocher-Homji, born into a Parsi (Zoroastrian Persian) family of Bombay (now Mumbai) in 1912. She worked with Bombay Talkies, a pioneering film company of that period. She was perhaps the first woman music director in the history of cinema, and a young one at that.

One by one the houses in Mihijam emptied. We too returned to Calcutta at the end of July 1943.

RASHBEHARI AVENUE

A pall of uncertainty, bordering on gloom, hung over Calcutta in 1943. There were probably several reasons for this. It was the aftermath of the crushing of the Quit India uprising. Hundreds of thousands of people were incarcerated across the country. The war was almost at the city's doorstep, on the India–Burma frontier. As if this was not cause enough for depression, huge numbers of starving people from rural Bengal started to flood into the city in the second half of 1943. The great Bengal famine of 1943–1944 was underway.

The liveliness had gone out of our Dover Lane neighbourhood as well. Some houses in the neighbourhood and across the city were still empty, their inhabitants having panicked at the prospect of Japanese bombs. Finally in December the Japanese air force did bomb Calcutta. As I recall, Japanese bombers first conducted a daytime raid and came back at night for another run. The attacks targeted only the Kidderpore docks area, where there were a lot of supply depots for the Allied war effort. In retrospect, it's clear that the attacks were almost token in nature. The Japanese were not going to do anything that might cause loss of life among ordinary Indians, and that too in the city of their valued ally Subhas Chandra Bose.

Nonetheless, the long-awaited appearance of Japanese planes in Calcutta's skies deepened the city's mood of insecurity. Air raid sirens would sound often, and no one really knew what might

happen. During the first, daytime attack on the Kidderpore docks Mother and I were home alone; Father was at work. Father began to feel that our English-style bungalow at 7/1 Dover Lane was not secure enough. It had a lot of big glass doors and windows which would shiver and shake whenever the sirens went off. They would certainly shatter from bomb vibrations. So he started to look for a new address in Calcutta to call home.

Around this time we had a family crisis as well. My father's younger brother, Uncle Manmatha, suffered a nervous breakdown and needed psychiatric treatment. Uncle Manmatha was very talented and highly qualified, an engineer at the Tata industrial complex in Jamshedpur. His illness hit us all very hard. Padmalaya, his wife, was then expecting a child. She came to stay with us at

ABOVE: *Bengal Famine (1943)*

Dover Lane and was then sent to Delhi to stay at Uncle Nirad's. A well-known Calcutta psychiatrist was treating Uncle Manmatha. Uncle Benode—my youngest paternal uncle—would take him to the psychiatrist's chamber, where he would be given electric shocks in the head! That was the conventional treatment for mental health problems then. I would feel very sad when Uncle Benode brought Uncle Manmatha to our house on Dover Lane after the visits to the doctor. Uncle Manmatha could barely walk and would lie down as soon as he could—he was in a zombie-like state. It was hard to watch. I was close to all my paternal uncles and all of them doted on me. Even though I was barely thirteen, I felt that the treatment was making his condition worse not better. But there was little to do except pray. Because of Father's atheist beliefs religious rituals were more or less banned in our house. As dusk fell women in the neighbouring houses would blow conch shells as part of their pujas. At that moment I would silently pray to the Almighty to cure my stricken uncle. He gradually did recover and later even went to Japan for advanced training in engineering.

Despite all the problems in our inner and outer worlds it was an exciting time to step into my teenage years. I read the newspapers carefully and listened regularly to the radio. When Gandhiji went on hunger strike in prison I announced that I would fast in solidarity. Father said, 'I will join you.' We fasted for a day and broke our fast with fruits Mother gave us in the evening. On that particular occasion the British government thought that Gandhi, advanced in age, might actually die. The government had even prepared a plan of how the news of his demise would be broadcast on All India Radio. But Gandhi, wily as always, broke his fast with fruit juice at a time of his choosing.

Father soon found a new address for us. We didn't move far, just to another part of south Calcutta's Ballygunge area. The address: 190C Rashbehari Avenue. We rented a spacious, airy flat occupying the entire top floor of a newly built four-storey apartment building overlooking Rashbehari Avenue, a major

Above: *Rashbehari Avenue today (October 2014)*

boulevard of south Calcutta. The tram line ran along the entire length of the boulevard; it still does. At that time and for several decades afterwards Rashbehari Avenue was primarily a well-off residential area. In recent years the long, wide boulevard has become lined with a new breed of flashy shops and stores, especially on the ground floors of former residential buildings. But some of the old, modest neighbourhood shops that have been doing business for many decades are still there.

Gariahat—one of Calcutta's leading shopping areas, then as now—was just a ten to fifteen-minute walk along the Avenue from our new home. Gariahat is a prime location to pick up everything from fresh fish and vegetables to saris and children's clothes. To the rear of our building the picturesque lakes of south Calcutta—a tree-shaded area excellent for morning or evening strolls—was just a short walk as well. Many think the Avenue is named after Rashbehari Bose, a freedom fighter who fled to Japan after World War I and turned over the leadership of the Indian independence movement in Southeast Asia to Netaji in 1943. However, it's actually named after Sir Rashbehari Ghose (1845–1921), a lawyer and philanthropist who was also president of the Indian National Congress during the first decade of the twentieth century. A political 'moderate', he was knighted by the British in 1915.

Father probably found our new home through Mother's family. The flats on the lower floors of 190C Rashbehari Avenue housed the administrative offices of Bengal Lamp, the firm set up at the initiative of my mother's father and run by her brothers. Father, a lawyer at the Calcutta high court, was on the board of directors of Bengal Lamp as the firm's legal adviser. The Bengal Lamp factory was in Jadavpur, a southern suburb, but the administration had moved into this newly built building in the heart of south Calcutta. So during the day the floors below us would teem with employees and activity. *Durwan*s (doormen) were on duty at the building's gate at night. Father's security concerns were satisfied. We were simply told to come down to a 'shelter' on the ground floor whenever the air raid siren went off.

In early 1944 we moved into 190C Rashbehari Avenue. Dover Lane was left behind, but memories lingered in my heart. I missed the guava tree in a corner of our garden; I used to climb that often with my playmates. The neighbouring garden belonging to Aunt Indu's house also carried memories. There was a hibiscus shrub in one corner that produced a flower known as *sthala padma* (land lotus). In another corner stood a *peepal* tree, sacred in Hinduism. One day a dog was found under that tree with her litter of four puppies. I took one of the pups home to raise as a pet. Just before we left Dover Lane it got run over by a military truck on the street. I was devastated. The grief inspired my first literary expression, an essay called '*Pather Kukur*' (The Stray Dog). That was the first time I realised that writing provided me with an outlet for my emotions, especially emotions which made the heart heavy.

'*Pather Kukur*' was published in the inaugural issue of our family magazine '*Lekhon*' (The Word). We used to get the popular

Bengali children's magazine '*Mouchak*' (The Beehive) at home; my parents had taken out a subscription for me. I especially liked the detective stories for children written by Hemendra Kumar Roy published in '*Mouchak*'. The characters were the private investigator, Jayanta, his sidekick, Manik, and the police inspector, Sundarbabu, who would constantly say 'Hmmm'. It was similar to the Poirot, Hastings and Inspector Japp triumvirate of the Agatha Christie books of the same period. Anyway, '*Mouchak*' gave me an idea—how about bringing out our own handwritten family magazine? I approached my cousins—Uncle Nirad's sons, Dhruva and Kirti, who were in Delhi, and another paternal uncle, Hiranmoy kaka's children, Chinmoy, Uttara and Sabita, who were in Calcutta—for contributions. Uncle Manmatha and Aunt Padmalaya also contributed under pseudonyms.

Thanks to Uncle Benode, who worked in publishing, the magazine did not have to come out in handwritten form. He got copies printed from Calcutta's Gouranga Press. The first issue was released while we were still at Dover Lane. The second and final issue had a ceremonial launch at our new Rashbehari Avenue residence. A host of relatives from both sides of the family—Roys and Chaudhuris—attended the launch, and Mother served up high tea. Even Aunt Anna, who could not read Bengali, took a copy.

Although our Rashbehari Avenue flat lacked its own green space, we gained a cultural environment that was perhaps the richest of any city in India at that time. In the 1940s the part of south Calcutta centred on Rashbehari Avenue was like a colony of artists, writers and scholars. On Hindustan Park the poet-couple Narendra Dev and Radharani Devi lived in their house 'Bhalobasha'. They were often compared to the nineteenth-century English poet-couple Robert Browning and Elizabeth Barrett Browning. We had a personal connection to them. Radharani Devi used to call my maternal grandfather, Lalit Roy, 'Baba'. She had been widowed at a young age and my grandfather, a fervent proponent of remarriage of young widows, was instrumental in getting her re-married. One of my sweetest childhood memories is the party they hosted on the first birthday of their daughter Nabaneeta. I was about six I think; we still lived on Dover Lane. It was a children's party in the Western style, with lots of fun games. All the kids who came went home with their own presents. Nabaneeta became a fine writer herself. She is also the first wife of the economist Amartya Sen.

At 202 Rashbehari Avenue was 'Kabita Bhaban', the residence of another celebrated writer-couple, Buddhadev Bose (1908–1974) and his wife Pratibha Bose. The sculptor Pradosh Dasgupta, later curator of the National Gallery of Modern Art in Delhi, lived nearby on Sardar Shankar Road with his wife Kamala, who was from Kerala in south India. He set up his studio on the ground floor of our building. The music composer and singer Sachin Dev Burman and his wife Meera would often be seen walking on Rashbehari Avenue. They lived on a narrow street off the Avenue almost opposite our building. This was just before Sachin Dev Burman moved to Bombay. Gopal Ghose (1913–1980), an innovative painter of landscapes, also lived in the neighbourhood. In 1943 he, Pradosh Dasgupta and a few others had founded the 'Calcutta Group', India's first collective of modernist artists. Gopal and Pradosh, young men at the time, became very attached to my father, whom they addressed as Charuda (older brother). They constantly dropped in at our flat. I remember Father saying about Gopal Ghose, 'A genius, but he drinks way too much.'

Also close by, on Bondel Road in the lakes area, lived Atul Bose (1898–1977), an eminent portrait painter. He was of East Bengal origin, born in Mymensingh. We used to visit his house often. Around this time I also met the famous painter Jamini Roy (1887–1972) for the first time. One of Abanindranath Tagore's first pupils, he was inspired by European impressionism in his early career but then moved to an original style based on the folk and tribal arts of Bengal (including the Kalighat *pat* tradition). On that first occasion I accompanied Father to his studio in Shyambazar in north Calcutta. Later he became our neighbour when he built a residence-cum-studio on Ballygunge Place, a nearby street. On Hindustan Park was 'Sudharma', the residence of Suniti Kumar Chatterji (1890–1977), the eminent linguist (in a sign of changing times, a part of this house is now a Fabindia store). He was a friend of Uncle Nirad's. It was only when I became an adult that I realised what an extraordinary collection of people formed our milieu at Rashbehari Avenue.

My most striking first memories of life on Rashbehari Avenue are however not of poets, painters and scholars. During the first half of 1944 Calcutta was flooded with destitute and dying people from villages across Bengal, the victims of the Bengal famine of 1943–1944. The windows of Father's spacious study in our third-floor flat overlooked the Avenue, one of Calcutta's prime boulevards. From those windows I would see long columns of terribly emaciated men, women and children, clad in rags, staggering down the Avenue begging for morsels of food. When I moved away from the windows, disturbed by the same sight day after day, week after week, I could still hear their haunting cries: '*Ektu phan dao Ma, ektu phan dao…*' (Mother, give us a little *phan*, just a little *phan*, please). In the traditional Bengali method of cooking rice, a very small quantity of water mixed with minute rice particles is left over in the utensil after the boiling process. This is known as phan. The rice is consumed and the phan is thrown away. The starving masses I saw and heard never asked for *bhat* (rice) or *khabar* (food). They only cried out for phan.

One day I saw a queue of these people in front of a house opposite our building. I noticed painfully thin young women, dressed in rags, some with naked infants in their arms. Soon the queue became unruly; people were pushing and shoving each other to get in front. Mother said, 'They are giving out loaves of bread from that house.' Almost opposite our building was Deshapran Mistanna Bhandar, a traditional Bengali sweet shop. Its display cabinets were stocked with *sandesh*, *rosogolla*, *amriti*—mouth-watering Bengali sweets and desserts. The columns would pause in front of the shop and stare at the display. Curiously, no one tried to loot. Were they too scared, or just too physically weak and mentally broken? Then they resumed their ghostly walk along Rashbehari Avenue, calling out for phan. Every day there were corpses on the Avenue, as people fell down and could not get up again. Others simply curled up on the pavement or in the gutters and died there.

The best scholarly studies of the Bengal famine of 1943–1944—by the American Paul Greenough and the Indian Amartya Sen, among others—have put the number who died at three to four million (of a total Bengal population of sixty million). It was a holocaust by hunger. These studies have also shown that the famine was man-made, a direct consequence of British wartime policies. The amazing thing is that even after the magnitude of the unfolding catastrophe had become clear—at the latest by autumn 1943—the colonial government made absolutely no effort to provide relief to the distressed.

Many years later I was sitting in the India Office Library archives in London, looking at papers related to the wartime activities of Subhas Chandra Bose. Netaji proclaimed the Provisional Government of Free India (*Arzi Hukumat-e Azad Hind* in Hindustani) in Singapore on 21 October 1943. Even before that, in August 1943, Netaji became concerned at the conditions in rural Bengal and communicated to the British government of India that he wished to send emergency supplies of rice by ship from Burma to Bengal. He wanted an assurance that the ships would not be attacked. The response of the British government is there in the archival records—they were very anxious to ensure that news of the offer did not reach the public in India. Indeed, the British were very good at suppressing information that did not suit them. They effectively suppressed the deaths of several million people from starvation—for which they were responsible as the occupying colonial power—from becoming known in the world. Even today the Bengal famine is little known in the wider world. Until the English East India Company established its writ over Bengal after the mid-eighteenth century, Bengal was a prosperous land, strong in agriculture and an important centre of the global maritime trade. From the time the British gained control of Bengal famine became a recurrent feature of life; the 1943–1944 famine was the last episode. Just before quitting the subcontinent, the colonial power took the lives of millions in the province where resistance to imperialism had caused them so much trouble since the beginning of the twentieth century.

My husband Sisir's memoirs of his own life during World War II contains an interesting anecdote that just came to mind. In autumn 1944 Sisir was being transferred from his underground cell at Delhi's Red Fort, where he had been briefly imprisoned, to the Lahore Fort, where he then had a particularly harrowing time. He was walking along the platform at the railway station in Delhi in handcuffs, flanked by armed guards. The station was full of the usual rush and hubbub; passengers and porters were scurrying about in all directions. As he walked along the crowded platform, he suddenly felt very lonely. Everyone was going about their mundane business and no one cared that a slender youth, obviously a political prisoner, was being taken somewhere by his captors. No one took any interest in him or gave him a second look. He wondered: Did Indians not care that a liberation army had breached the north-eastern borders of India, that the army's helpers inside India, people such as himself, were risking so much for the country's freedom? That they did care became clear once the story of the INA became known to the public in India in autumn 1945, after the end of World War II. But until then they had no clue.

ABOVE: *Sisir Kumar Bose (1955)*

British censorship and disinformation had suppressed the story, just like the story of mass starvation in Bengal.

Whilst all these historic events were taking place, a big development happened in my own life. After years of home schooling, I finally started going to school! I was thirteen. The Ballygunge Girls' School was a walk of twenty minutes or so from our Rashbehari Avenue address. It had a recently arrived headmistress, Manorama Bose. Manorama Auntie was a childhood friend of Mother's from Dhaka. She told Father that as my 'matric' (school-leaving) examinations were less than three years away it was important that I be enrolled in a school as soon as possible. The ninth and tenth grades of school were the build-up to the examinations, but as I would need to adjust to the school atmosphere I should be enrolled in the eighth grade without delay. Father was persuaded.

I would walk to school from home. After crossing the wide Rashbehari Avenue I would take a narrow street next to the sweet shop and then take Hindustan Road. I would pass Aunt Indu and Uncle Hem's house at the corner of Hindustan Road and Dover Lane. It was a pleasant walk, along calm streets with two-storey houses inhabited by upper-middle-class Bengali families. One of the houses belonged to Sunayani Devi (1875–1962), a member of the Tagore family and a self-taught painter of distinction. She had been married at the age of eleven to a grandson of Raja Ram Mohan Roy, the famous social reform advocate of Bengal in the early nineteenth century. Some of those houses are still there, while others have been demolished in recent years and replaced by apartment complexes. At first Ram Lakhan, one of the doormen in our building, would escort me to school. After a while I walked there and back on my own.

Manorama Auntie was a serious sort but not intimidating. But the deputy headmistress Sumatidi was a bit of a dragon. The girls were scared of her. She was also the English teacher. She decreed that only English would be spoken during her English classes. The class went silent as a result. It was a Bengali-medium school and none of the girls were proficient in conversational English. Sumatidi was walking around the classroom during an English grammar lesson. As a new girl, I had been allocated a desk at the back of the room. Sumatidi stopped in front of my desk and asked me in an angry tone, 'Why don't you have the grammar book?' I was not used to speaking English, but because of Father's extensive personal library of books by authors from all over the world either written in or translated into English I was well-read in the language and could write it reasonably well. So my confidence level was slightly higher than the other girls. I stood up and replied, 'The book is out of print. I checked with the publisher and they said there will be a delay in getting it. My father has asked the publisher to be as quick as possible.'

Sumatidi glared at me. Then she said, 'Gather up your things.' I was frightened now but all she did was to put me in a desk in the front row. It was a form of recognition, and was good for my morale. But I still managed to make blunders. During the half-yearly examinations we had to write answers to four questions on the history paper. After writing three answers my hand started aching so I didn't write the fourth. I was used to home schooling, where I stopped writing as soon as I felt tired.

Another teacher with a strong personality was Malatidi, the history teacher. Our history textbook was *Swadesh o Sabhyata* (Our Land and Civilisation) written by Kalidas Nag. Kalidas Nag (1891–1966) was one of a generation of Indian historians who emerged in Bengal in the 1920s concurrently with the national awakening of that decade, when the struggle for India's freedom became a mass movement. Ramesh Chandra (R.C.) Majumdar (1888–1980) was another example of this generation. Malatidi would require us to memorise entire chapters of *Swadesh o Sabhyata* for class. She would then pick on students at random to test whether they had done so. It was hard, but later I was grateful for Malatidi's strict regimen. *Swadesh o Sabhyata* is no ordinary textbook. It's a minor classic that provides a wonderful survey of India from antiquity to the early twentieth century. I liked its treatment of the Mughal period but the period since the British arrival interested me the most. I noticed how Nag subtly differentiated between the British officials who governed India. Lord Curzon, the man who tried to partition Bengal in the first decade of the twentieth century was portrayed in an unflattering light but Lord Bentinck, governor-general of India from 1828 to 1835, received a more sympathetic treatment due to his efforts to outlaw *sati*, the practice of burning Hindu women alive on the funeral pyre of their deceased husbands.

In the half-yearly examinations I came third in my class, to my amazement. In the year-end examinations I came first. After that I came first with monotonous regularity. Our relatives and family friends were pleasantly surprised by my success in school. Looking back later in life, I realised that perhaps it wasn't so surprising after all. I was a bookworm, a distinctly academic type who would regularly spend hours with the books in my bibliophile father's library.

My greatest gain from school was however making friends my own age. I slowly emerged from the introverted shell of my only-child existence. It was a gradual and tentative process. I was too shy to approach others. So my friendships were formed with those who approached me.

It was not that I was completely isolated before I started going to school. I had lots of paternal and maternal cousins. On my mother's side I was younger than most of my cousins because my mother was sixth of eight children—five boys and three girls. Only two brothers—Kiran, who married Aunt Anna, the American, and Bimal—were younger than her. My father, on the other hand, was the eldest of eight siblings—six brothers and two sisters. So I was *didi* (older sister) to a bunch of paternal cousins. But this small army of paternal and maternal cousins were not part of my daily existence. I would see them from time to time.

Some of those occasions were great fun. Once a year all members of my mother's family present in Calcutta would convene for a family dinner at Uncle Kiran and Aunt Anna's flat on Theatre Road (now Shakespeare Sarani, and still a posh street in central Kolkata). Aunt Anna would move the sofas from the living room and everybody would sit on the floor and eat together. My favourite was the *moong* dal cooked with fish head, and of course the chutney at the end of the main meal. When *doi*—Bengali-style sweet yoghurt—was served some of the guests would playfully squabble over who would get the *matha* (head), the delectable upper crust. Aunt Anna was quite puzzled why people were fighting over the 'upper portion', as she called it. Only native Bengalis usually understand this sort of thing.

ABOVE: *Aunt Anna and Phul mama (mid 1930s)*

Mother's eldest sister had five daughters. I was closest to the youngest, Lebudi, who was four years older than me. At one of these gatherings she said to me, 'Let's imagine we have all got together like this twenty years from now.' I tried to imagine what it would be like but it was difficult to visualise the future at that age. Finally Lebudi said, 'You are married. With three children. And you are really fat.' I dissolved in giggles. She continued, 'And I'm unmarried. A typical thin and bitter spinster.' We both doubled up in laughter. Later I did have three children, though I didn't become too fat. Lebudi—her name was Shobha—became a doctor. She married Sunil Janah (1918–2012), one of India's finest photographers of the twentieth century. His work first became known through his photographs of the suffering of the 1943–1944 famine in Bengal. He quickly became known as a socially committed photographer who travelled deep into rural India to document the condition of the people, particularly hunger.

A photograph of me and Sisir he took during a chaperoned visit to his and Lebudi's house in Calcutta in autumn 1955, just before our marriage, is a cherished item in our family archives.

My happy memories of 14 Theatre Road end at the age of fourteen. Phul mama (Uncle Kiran) died suddenly and tragically while climbing in the eastern Himalayas in autumn 1945. I describe what happened towards the end of this chapter. After his death the address on Theatre Road passed from our lives. Years later Uncle Bimal—Mother's youngest brother—set up home there with his wife, Aunt Dolly, and their children. They brought my maternal grandmother to live with them in her last years. So I was a regular visitor to the spacious flat on Theatre Road for well over three decades after my marriage. Those visits have long ended but today I often pass the stately building on Shakespeare Sarani by car.

At Ballygunge Girls' School I soon made a 'best friend'—Kumkum. The reason we became close is that she took the initiative to make friends with me. Unused to the school environment, I was too shy and tongue-tied to approach anyone on my own. Kumkum was a lovely person. She was not very good at her studies, and would take great pride in my academic achievements. I would tell her to concentrate more on her studies, to absolutely no avail. She would come running towards me on the school verandah, literally jumping with joy, 'The results of the English exam are out! You got 77 [out of 100 marks], first in class!' 'How about you,' I asked. 'I scored 40.' 'Then why are you jumping so much?' 'Why, because you have come first!' Kumkum always remembered my birthday and gave me a small gift every year. She was married off when I was in college. She was still relatively young when she died of cancer in the late 1970s.

Below: *Kumkum, Krishna's closest friend at school (late 1940s)*

The group vibe was friendly at school, but there were pairs of 'besties' as well.

The best-friend pairs would often be referred to together: Krishna and Kumkum, Mira and Ila, and so on. My friendships with Mira, Ila, Kumkum and others continued long after school. In the tenth grade new friends joined our circle: Jayanti, Madhavi and others. I remember Jayanti fell ill and was in a sanatorium for a while. We used to correspond through letters. Madhavi's maternal grandfather was Benimadhab Bezbaruah, a well-known professor of ancient Indian languages. She used to live at his home with her mother. Her father was not around. Some of the girls would tease her about her father's absence. She would reply that he had gone to Europe to study and could not return because of the outbreak of World War II. After school I lost touch with Madhavi. We met again in the 1980s when I was the principal of a women's college in Calcutta and she was the principal of another women's college in the city.

I met Madhavi's 'missing' father several times during the intervening decades, in Europe and in India. The first time was in Paris in 1960, and later in that decade I met him in Bombay and Calcutta as well. He was Girija Mukherjee, who worked closely with Netaji in Germany in 1942. He was permanently settled in Europe, with a German wife whom he had married during World War II and their daughter. Whenever I met him he would wax rhapsodic on the grace and beauty of Bengali women, who according to him had no peer in the world. I told Sisir, 'Perhaps he's been away from Bengal a bit too long.'

In the mid-1960s Sisir invited him to Calcutta to deliver the 'Netaji Oration'. This is an address given annually at Netaji Bhawan on 23rd January, Netaji's birthday, by a person who has some special insight into Netaji's life and work—as a colleague or a scholar. Girija Mukherjee gave an exceptionally insightful address. The next day all the papers in Calcutta front-paged his speech along with pictures. A day or two later Sisir finished seeing his patients in his chamber in our Woodburn Park residence and found a young couple waiting to speak to him—a woman and her husband. He told me, looking rather worried, that the woman was very keen to meet Girija Mukherjee. I said, 'That must have been Madhavi.' He said, 'What? You know her?'

When some of the girls in our school in 1946 would taunt Madhavi about her absent father, she would reply with great pride that her father, an expatriate in Europe, had joined Netaji Subhas Chandra Bose and assisted him in his struggle for India's freedom.

Our school had a vibrant extra-curricular side. Music and theatre were the two staples. The star performer at musical events was Sumitradi, who studied one class above me. As Sumitra Sen, she became one of the best-known singers of Rabindra sangeet. Her daughters Indrani Sen and Srabani Sen are also popular singers.

I was considered good at elocution, so would be part of the cast in school plays. Once I played Marcus Antonius (Mark Antony) in a performance of Shakespeare's *Julius Caesar*. At Father's suggestion I draped a white *chador* (stole) around my shoulders in an improvisation of the Roman toga. By that time a college section had been added to our school. Its first principal was Sujata Ray, a well-known educationist. She came to see our dress-rehearsal. I declaimed, 'Friends, Romans, Countrymen, lend me your ears. I come to bury Caesar not to praise him.' She was impressed. When she heard that my father had tutored me for the role she said, 'Oh, he must have spent quite some time in England.' I didn't divulge that not only had my father never been to England, he and his brothers had learned English at home in a small East Bengal town called Kishoregunj.

Next I got the title role in a performance of *Macbeth*. I walked on to stage wielding a blood-stained knife—made from *rangta* (shiny foil) and daubed with *alta* (red dye)—and announced, 'I have done the deed.' My mother was in the audience with Uncle Manmatha's little son in her lap. He started shrieking 'Didi! Didi!' in great excitement. The audience erupted in laughter.

Despite these public performances—once I also sang north Indian classical music at a school event—the nervousness of my nature never left me. This was undoubtedly the result of being an only child who did not go to school till the age of thirteen. I would get stage fright before all my appearances. I was also scared of examinations, and would regularly panic when they approached. This persisted into my adult life—I had a meltdown of sorts just before my MA examinations.

My training in music was rather sporadic. For some reason Father felt that I lacked singing talent. He would tell Mother, 'She won't be a good singer. She's like your family in that respect.' Mother would get angry. I received praise for my dancing abilities as a child but formal training in dance was out of the question—dancing in public was taboo for girls of our social class beyond pre-teen years. Because Father's family was steeped in music, especially Rabindra sangeet, I did receive lessons off and on from Father as well as Uncle Manmatha. For a while I was taught by Benoy kaka, a friend of Father's who was from Mymensingh. He would play the organ as he taught me to sing. Later in life, whenever I ran into him he would remind me that he had been my music teacher. Benoy Uncle's son, Chandrodoy, married Mamata Shankar, the daughter of the famed dancers Uday Shankar and Amala Shankar. Mamata—I call her 'Momo'—is herself an accomplished dancer as well as an actress.

Kuntala Auntie, a distant aunt of mine through marriage into my mother's family, came to visit Calcutta from her home in Allahabad. She was an excellent singer. At that time Allahabad was the main centre of music in north India. Mother and Kuntala Auntie decided to go to the movies, to watch *Shesh Uttar* (The Final Answer), directed by the legendary filmmaker and actor Pramathesh Barua (1903–1951) and starring Barua and Kanan Devi in the lead roles. They wanted to take me along. Father objected as he thought the movie might be unsuitable for children. Eventually he relented after an argument. *Shesh Uttar*, released in 1942, was Barua's last great film—he wasted away from alcoholism after that. Its Hindi version, *Jawaab*, was also a big success.

little platform under a tin roof. Ghoom is a very fog-prone place and that adds to the atmosphere. We would board the toy train at Ghoom and pass through the Batasia Loop, where the line does a spiral, to Darjeeling. After strolling and shopping in Darjeeling we would walk back to Ghoom along one of the two walking paths between the Darjeeling mall and Ghoom—Calcutta Road and Auckland Road. The Calcutta Road is featured in one of Rabindranath Tagore's short stories. In it a lovelorn princess from a north Indian Muslim family sits on a boulder on the mist-shrouded Calcutta Road, pining for her Hindu lover. Set in the aftermath of the Great Revolt of 1857, it is one of Tagore's finest short stories.

Humayun Kabir (1906–1969), a family friend who became a major political figure in West Bengal in the 1960s, was staying at a house on Auckland Road with his wife, Shanti, and their two children, Pasha and Leila. They would often come over to Balaclava to have breakfast. I still remember the smell of eggs and sausages frying in Aunt Anna's kitchen. Leila was very small, she would spend her time picking cherries in the garden. Later she was Leila Fernandes, wife of the charismatic political leader George Fernandes. Pasha liked subjecting me to quizzes. One day he asked me, 'How high is the horizon?' I was nonplussed. He said, 'It's as high as you can see with your eyes.'

There was a cottage nearly opposite Balaclava, but at a slightly lower elevation. Here Suhrid Sinha, a major zamindar of the Mymensingh district in East Bengal, was holidaying with his wife and little daughter. Mrs Sinha had been educated at Tagore's university in Santiniketan. We got

BELOW: *Ghoom, Darjeeling district (1944). Krishna's Uncle Kiran is doffing his hat on the far left*

on very well with them and their little daughter became quite attached to me. I would tell her stories. When we met she said, 'I am Suchhanda Sinha, what is your name?' I replied, 'You are *sinha* [lion] and I am *piprey* [ant].' She would call me 'piprey' from then on.

Our sojourn at Balaclava was idyllic, with one small problem. Balaclava was on the route from Darjeeling to Tiger Hill, where generations of tourists to Darjeeling have travelled to catch the best view of the Kanchenjunga range at sunrise. So there was some disturbance from the tourist traffic, and that too at an early hour.

Suddenly one day my Uncle Khirode—Father's younger brother, the paediatrician Dr K.C. Chaudhuri—turned up at Balaclava. He wanted to go trekking in the mountains of the Darjeeling district. Uncle Kiran, an avid mountaineer, was all for it. It was decided to form two separate trekking teams. Uncle Kiran, Aunt Anna and a few of their friends would trek to the Nathu-La Pass, perched at 14,000 feet above sea level on the border between Sikkim and Tibet. Father, Mother, Uncle Khirode and Uncle Khirode's friend Sachin Sarbadhikari, also a physician, would do a shorter trek to Sandakphu and Phalut, the highest peaks in the Darjeeling Himalayas perched at 12,500 feet above sea level on the border with Sikkim. There was an intense discussion about what to do with me. Kirkin, our mountain guide from the Sherpa community of the eastern Nepal Himalayas, said that it would be too risky to take a *chhoti ladki* (small girl) on an expedition deep into the Himalayas. I was approaching my fourteenth birthday, but was both short and of slight build. Eventually the adults decided I would be taken along, because I could not be left on my own in Ghoom or Darjeeling. Kirkin did not know that I was a good walker; the morning walks with my parents had prepared me well for the challenges of Himalayan trekking.

The first stop after Ghoom was a village called Manebhanjang. Nowadays there are motorable roads in the area, but back then walking or riding on horseback were the only ways of getting

ABOVE: *At a forest bungalow in the Darjeeling hills while trekking (1944). Krishna with her parents and her uncle Dr K.C. Chaudhuri (standing)*

around. After Manebhanjang the trek got challenging; a lot of ascents and descents brought us to the next stop, the village of Tonglu. After a steep uphill climb the path would descend into a valley. In these little valleys there were tiny hamlets, each with a few families. Livestock grazed outside the dwellings, next to pea-fields. Mother would talk to the women. Extremely friendly, they picked peas for us to eat. The sweetest and freshest peas I have tasted in my life. Then we would tackle the next ascent. When we reached the travellers' bungalow at Tonglu for the overnight halt, Uncle Khirode announced that we were now more than 10,000 feet above sea level and altitude sickness was a possibility. He asked if anyone had a headache or was feeling any other discomfort.

My head was already throbbing, but I kept quiet. But after a while it got worse—it was as if horses were racing, hooves thudding, inside my head. Kirkin was unfazed. He brought me warm pea-soup in bed and put a hot-water bottle on my feet. 'Just lie down for a while and it will go away,' he said.

Balaclava was visible from the bungalow at Tonglu. We had agreed with our neighbours, the Sinhas, that we would focus torches in their direction from Tonglu and they would do the same from Ghoom. We did see lights flickering around Balaclava but it may have been the headlights of cars on the Hill Cart Road.

The next morning my headache was gone and we set out for Sandakphu from Tonglu. I noticed that the surroundings were becoming desolate, with less and less vegetation. The mountain-tops we crossed were rather bare but we encountered forests of pine during the descents. The mountain tracks were snaky, full of hairpin bends. We frequently encountered cascading waterfalls. Sometimes we would cross waterfalls wedged between two hills on precarious, swaying foot-bridges. We took a few coffee breaks. Uncle Khirode poured milky coffee from his flask for everyone to share. Of the eight Chaudhuri siblings—six brothers and two sisters—he was the only one who did not sing or play an instrument. But sipping coffee underneath pine trees by a raging waterfall even he broke into off-key Rabindra sangeet.

We had two sturdy horses with us. Anyone who felt tired was welcome to take a horse ride. Mother was doing so quite frequently! I noticed Mother was really at ease riding the horses. She just adjusted the way she wore her sari a bit and then rode along smartly. Once, after a fairly long descent we stopped at a roadside tea-stall to have some tea. A few European trekkers came down the *chora bato*—short cut in the local tongue—in front of us. They smiled at us and said, 'What are you enjoying? Arrack?' Everyone laughed. There was no need for intoxicants. The experience we were having in the lap of the Himalayas was intoxicating enough.

BELOW: *Krishna's mother Chhaya Devi Chaudhurani on horseback in the Darjeeling Himalayas (1944)*

As soon as we reached the bungalow at the tiny village of Sandakphu Mother took over the kitchen there. Everyone was hungry after a long day's trek. When steaming hot chicken curry and pulao rice appeared on the dining table Uncle Khirode was ecstatic, 'Thank God, we brought Boudi along!'

The route from Sandakphu to Phalut was quite barren of vegetation. A path carved from rock with mountains on either side. The peaks on one side were covered with clouds and on the other side brilliantly illuminated by sunlight. Amid this play of clouds and the sun we arrived at the travellers' bungalow in Phalut. Mother immediately commandeered the kitchen again, with Kirkin in the assistant's role. I had noticed that the bungalows all had visitors' books. Most of the visitors over the years were either British or from countries of Europe. Leafing through the visitors' book at Phalut I saw that one visitor, an Englishman, had criticised the bungalow's furniture. The next day another Englishman had written, 'Fool, did you expect the Grand Hotel here?'

At Sandakphu, we were not quite on the roof of the world, but certainly on the roof of Bengal. At nearly 12,500 feet, Sandakphu is the highest point in Bengal (Phalut is at a marginally lower altitude). Sandakphu is still a popular destination for trekking groups, most of whom are drawn there by the grand vista of the eastern Himalayas the point commands. At sunrise I saw a sight I remember vividly seventy years later. A string of peaks—among them four of the world's five highest peaks, Everest, Kanchenjunga, Lhotse and Makalu—appeared majestically in front of us. The summit of Mount Everest was the first to be touched by the rays of the sun, then the sunlight spread within minutes to swathe all the virgin-white peaks in a crimson glow. A spectacle out of this world. It was awesome and strangely humbling at the same time; one felt an unknown, unfathomable, unearthly presence at work somewhere.

From Phalut we commenced a steep descent back to Ghoom, but along a different route from the one we had taken to come up. The return journey took us through the pretty hamlets of Rammam and Rimbick. This route meandered through thick forests. Sometimes we would walk beside a gurgling *chu* (mountain stream), and once or twice we crossed one across a wooden bridge. The ascent had been too arduous to sing. Now I broke into song as we walked along. Mother and Dr Sarbadhikari took recourse to the horses from time to time. Father, Uncle Khirode and I walked the whole way. The forest bungalows where we stopped overnight were just beautiful. I especially remember the bungalow deep inside the forest at a hamlet called Batasi, in front of which we took a group photograph. Here, at somewhat lower altitudes, it was less cold and we sat on the covered verandahs in the evenings. I would sing as the moonlight cast a gentle glow on the pine forests.

ABOVE: *During trekking, high in the Darjeeling Himalayas. Krishna and some local children (1944)*

A few days after we returned to Ghoom, Uncle Kiran, Aunt Anna and their party too returned safe and sound from the expedition to the Nathu-La Pass. We had all returned to civilisation. Or was it really civilisation? In our idyll in the mountains of Darjeeling in October 1944 we were cocooned from the savage warfare sweeping much of the world as World War II entered its climactic phase. But there were reminders. The mall in the centre of Darjeeling town was full of crowds of British and American soldiers. Aunt Anna and I both found the hordes of uniformed men scary. Occasionally American officers—gregarious and outgoing unlike their British counterparts—would speak to Aunt Anna and be thrilled to discover that she was American too. Aunt Anna didn't like the attention at all but a couple of times she felt obliged to invite them over for tea at Balaclava.

My greatest thrill was riding the toy train. I soon knew the names of all the stations. Sonada was just before Ghoom, Darjeeling just after. I always tried to get into the rear saloon, covered with glass. This offered unrestricted views of the hills, ravines, waterfalls and pine forests. In the 1990s the toy train service was suspended for the first time in well over one hundred years, due to the effect of the Gorkhaland agitation and other factors. When I was elected to my first term in Parliament in 1996, the politician Ram Vilas Paswan became the Union railways minister. One day he called a meeting in New Delhi of MPs from West Bengal to ask for suggestions. I made two requests. First: Could the Darjeeling Himalayan Railway be revived, please? Second: Could the Calcutta Metro station at Bhowanipur be named 'Netaji Bhavan' station? Paswan responded: *Ho jayega*—it will be done. I didn't believe him. He delivered on both requests.

When we returned to Calcutta in early November we found its streets also crowded with Allied soldiers. Most of them were American, including many black servicemen. To the rear of our Rashbehari Avenue address, by the lakes, a big barracks had been set up for the American servicemen. The lakes area, a leafy public park with water bodies, was where we would take our morning and evening walks. Sometimes Father and I would walk together, at other times I would be alone walking my dog Jimmy on a leash. An American soldier coming from the other direction would say 'Hello!' and extend his hand. Frightened out of my wits, I would scuttle to the pavement on the other side of the street, dragging surprised Jimmy after me. Father would nod curtly in acknowledgement. After dusk the soldiers were confined to the barracks. One evening my cousin Lebudi and I were walking together. Lebudi was carrying a fat book—four years older than me, she had just enrolled in Calcutta's Medical College. A soldier hailed us from across the iron railings that separated the barracks from the street, 'Hi, can I have a look at your book?' I was terrified and wanted to run away, but Lebudi was unfazed. She stopped and replied, 'Go and buy one!'

One of my friends at Ballygunge Girls' School told me that several American officers were billeted in a house next to theirs.

She said they were very nice. They had come over to her house for a meal and showed her family photographs of their families—the wives and children they had left behind in the United States. On the other hand, the barracks by the lakes were a magnet for Calcutta's sex-worker population. Off Southern Avenue, the long tree-lined road that runs by the lakes, American soldiers sprawled on the grass with Indian women were a common sight. The middle and upper-middle class society of our genteel south Calcutta neighbourhood pretended not to notice.

At this time there was heavy fighting going on in Burma, close to India's north-eastern frontier. The freedom movement inside India was at a low ebb. Since the brutal repression of the Quit India uprisings two years earlier, nationalist leaders and activists were either in prison or in hiding. But earlier that year, between March and July 1944, the Indian National Army had crossed into India alongside Japanese forces and fought bravely on the Imphal and Kohima fronts (in the present-day Indian states of Manipur and Nagaland, respectively). The exploits against great odds of Netaji Subhas Chandra Bose's soldiers were unknown to the people of India because of the efficient British censorship and disinformation machine.

In fact, in April 1944 the national tricolour had been raised for the first time on liberated soil on the Indian mainland by INA forces. The place was Moirang in Manipur, a town in the Imphal valley. The INA's Colonel Shaukat Malik raised the national flag there (earlier, in December 1943, Netaji raised the national tricolour on the Andaman and Nicobar Islands in the Indian Ocean). In the hills of Manipur, above the Imphal valley, the INA's First Division commanded by Mohammad Zaman Kiani had set up base for four months. On the Kohima front INA troops led by Shah Nawaz Khan fought with distinction. Amid torrential monsoon rains in July 1944 the INA forces started their retreat back into Burma. During that long retreat that stretched into the spring of 1945, INA forces fought with almost incredible tenacity in Burma—

under the command of Colonel Prem Kumar Sahgal in the Mount Popa area and Colonel Gurbaksh Singh Dhillon on the banks of the Irrawaddy river. None of this was known to ordinary Indians, who had access only to British war propaganda in the newspapers and on the radio.

Our daily life in Calcutta was dominated by other things, though. Uncle Kiran, a livewire by nature, would often provide a spark of excitement. One day he turned up at Rashbehari Avenue and announced that our flat would be the venue of a wedding. A wedding? It emerged that the bride-to-be was my cousin Kutidi, a daughter of Mother's eldest sister. A young man who was a friend of Kutidi's brother had fallen for her. He was the older of two sons of a prominent businessman, Adinath Sen, whose house on Ballygunge Place was close to our Rashbehari Avenue home. The Sens were fine with the proposed union and Kutidi's mother, my eldest maternal aunt, had no objections either. The problem was Kutidi's father. A resolute opponent of inter-caste marriage, he would certainly object to his daughter, a *kayastha*, marrying someone with the surname 'Sen', from the *vaidya* community. Therefore the wedding would have to be planned discreetly and presented as a *fait accompli* to the obdurate father. It was quite a conspiracy, albeit in a good cause. Kutidi's mother came to stay with us with her daughters. The groom-to-be—Debnath Sen, Chhokonda to me—would come by with his car and take Kutidi out on drives.

The date of the wedding approached. The furniture in Father's study and our adjoining living room was pushed back to the walls and the floor space covered with rugs for people to sit. The Sens arrived—Adinath, Debnath and Debnath's younger brother and sister, who became Tutuda and Sonadi to me. Then the marriage registrar arrived. While the formalities were completed I joined an impromptu choir singing love songs.

Then Kutidi's father walked in. A civil surgeon by profession, he had supervised my birth in Dhaka. Now he was posted in Bardhaman (or Burdwan as it was spelled then), a large town about sixty miles north-west of Calcutta. Informed that morning by telephone of his daughter's nuptials, he had taken the first available train to Calcutta. Judging by his body language and facial expression he was clearly not happy, but decorum prevailed and he didn't make a scene.

At that time in the mid-1940s and for two or three decades afterwards, one of the stock characters in Bengali movies was a fearsome father who would make no end of trouble over his daughter marrying a man of her own choice. The actors Pahari Sanyal and Chhabi Biswas played this role to perfection. The *filmi* father would invariably wear a silk dressing gown and pace up and down while fuming. After much melodrama, the movies would always end on a happy note as the patriarch would see reason and give in. Reconciliation and harmony would prevail. This film script played out right in front of my eyes. Uncle Kiran's madcap plan worked like a charm.

After this we were regular visitors to the Sens' Ballygunge Place residence for several years. There was a large pond on their property. Mother loved to swim; she had grown up swimming regularly in the lakes and ponds of the East Bengal countryside. The Sens' in-house pond became her and my swimming pool. A couple of years after Kutidi and Chhokonda's wedding in our Rashbehari Avenue flat, Chhokonda's younger brother, Tutuda—Dibanath Sen—also got married. His bride was Roma, an extremely pretty girl of sixteen from a cultured East Bengal family. Within a year Roma and Dibanath had a daughter. Kutidi would often visit us at Rashbehari Avenue carrying the bonny baby. Then Chhokonda took a job at a tea garden near Kurseong, in the Darjeeling district, and he and Kutidi left Calcutta. Thereafter our visits to the Sens' residence on Ballygunge Place ceased. A few years later, in the early 1950s, Roma became a subject of discussion amongst our relatives. She had done something unusual—very unusual indeed for a married woman with wealthy in-laws. She had started a career as an actress in the Bengali film industry. Roma took the more glamorous-sounding professional name Suchitra and became famous as Suchitra Sen, the Greta Garbo of Bengali cinema. Most of her biggest hits starred her opposite another iconic figure of Bengali cinema, the actor Uttam Kumar. The bonny baby I remember from the late 1940s also became an actress—Moon Moon Sen.

In 1945 I was in the ninth grade of school. The war in Europe ended in May, and in August the stubborn Japanese too capitulated in the wake of Hiroshima and Nagasaki. In India things were quiet—the freedom movement was barely active and nationalist prisoners started to be released only around the middle of the year.

Aunt Anna had not visited her home in the United States for twelve years, since coming to India in 1933. Her mother in Boston was aged and not keeping well. As the war wound down it was decided that she would make a trip to America. She went by ship, of course. It was a long journey of a few months.

Before she left she told Uncle Kiran not to go mountaineering. He had had a slightly alarming medical check-up with Dr Bidhan Roy, a renowned physician who was also a leader of the Congress party in Bengal. Dr Roy (1882–1962) would serve as West Bengal's chief minister from 1948 to 1962. During that time he became well-known as an advocate of industrialisation. Dr Roy knew Uncle Kiran, who was already established as a young industrialist, and liked him very much. Bengal Lamp was one of the leading Indian-owned enterprises of Bengal and MIT-educated Uncle Kiran was just the kind of person Dr Roy believed Bengal and India needed. During the check-up Dr Roy detected that something was not quite right with Uncle Kiran's respiratory system. There appeared to be a problem with one of his lungs. Further tests were needed but in the meantime Dr Roy told Uncle Kiran to cut down on his mountaineering, and especially to avoid very high altitudes.

After Aunt Anna left Uncle Kiran turned up one day at Rashbehari Avenue to speak to me. He said, 'Hey, want to go trekking with me? I'm going to Green Lake, at the base of

Kanchenjunga. It's more than 16,000 feet high.' I was thrilled to bits at the prospect of camping at the base of the world's third highest peak, close to Sikkim's border with Tibet. But Father vetoed my joining Uncle Kiran's adventure. Father said that this autumn we needed to go to Mihijam, to check on the upkeep of our holiday home in the Santhal Parganas if nothing else. I was depressed but there was nothing to do.

Father, Mother and I left for Mihijam once the Durga Puja vacation began. Aunt Anna was at sea. Uncle Kiran started for Green Lake—an arduous trek through the Sikkim Himalaya—with two friends, Mr Pandya and Mr Arindam Sen. He had heard very good things from us about Kirkin, the Sherpa guide who had accompanied us on our Darjeeling trek the previous autumn. So he took Kirkin along.

Once in Mihijam I soon forgot my unhappiness at missing out on the trip to Green Lake. It was simply delightful to return to this secluded place on the Bengal–Bihar border after a couple of years. I became busy with the chickens and the rabbits, and plucked fruit from the custard-apple tree. I watched our caretaker Gokul draw water from our courtyard well, and helped him to water the beds of roses in our blooming garden. Young Santhal women would come by our house and perform their distinctive dance.

One morning a telegram arrived. Father opened and read it. He put it in his pocket and immediately walked off somewhere at a rather brisk pace. He returned with three tickets for the next Calcutta-bound train. He told Mother there was an emergency in his office. Mother, trusting if not naïve by nature, was a little suspicious but believed him.

As soon as we walked in through the door of our top-floor flat on Rashbehari Avenue our long-time maid Sahachari whispered to me, 'Have you heard? Mamababu [uncle-sir] has died in the mountains.' I was stunned. I looked around quickly to see if Mother had heard. She hadn't. Father had. He said, 'Give her a little time.'

A little later Father broke the news to Mother. Mother was quite shattered. Of her seven siblings, Uncle Kiran was closest to her in age—he was just a couple of years younger to her—and they had grown up together and been extremely close all their lives. He was her favourite sibling, her darling little brother. Moreover we had grown to really treasure Anna, the wife he had brought home from America. Uncle Kiran's life had been cut short in the most untimely manner—he was in his early forties, the livewire of the family with a promising future ahead of him.

Soon our flat filled with people. My doctor uncle Khirode, Father's younger brother and himself an avid mountaineer, refused to give up hope. He told Mother, 'Boudi, not to worry. I'm leaving on a rescue mission tomorrow. He has fallen sick but I'm going to bring him back, come what may.'

It was a hollow hope. The next day word reached us that a rescue team from Darjeeling's Himalayan Mountaineering Institute had started out for the base of Kanchenjunga but been forced to turn back by heavy snowfall which made progress impossible. Most likely the area would not be accessible until the onset of the following summer.

Gradually we learned what had happened. Some of the information came from Uncle Kiran's companions, Mr Pandya and Mr Sen, and some from Uncle Kiran's diary, which they brought back for us. Uncle Kiran had been panting heavily during steep ascents and often fell behind the rest of the group. He was in clear discomfort during the final climb to Green Lake. Even at that altitude it can feel quite hot in the sun during ascents. He had taken off his pullover sweater while climbing and slung it over his shoulder. It fell off accidentally and he came down a few hundred feet to retrieve it before re-commencing the upward climb.

An entry in Uncle Kiran's diary read: 'I'll never bring this fellow Kirkin with me again. First he said, "*Saheb* [Sir] you are not well, let's turn back." Now he's saying he doesn't like the look of the sky, he thinks there might be a snowstorm. What a useless guide he is.'

As soon as the tents were pitched on Green Lake—an alpine meadow with a lovely little lake just below the Zemu glacier, which is at nearly 18,000 feet—Uncle Kiran lay down in one of them. The next morning he could not get up. Kirkin felt that this was nothing worse than altitude sickness. If Uncle Kiran could be brought down just a few hundred feet he would recover. The problem was that he could not stand up, let alone walk. So Kirkin sent the two other Sherpas downhill to fetch logs of wood. They would make a makeshift stretcher and carry him down.

In the afternoon the wind picked up significantly, then snow started to fall. Late in the afternoon another climber, a white man, appeared accompanied by a Sherpa. He said they planned to make camp a little further up and pushed on. Just after that the snowfall turned into a blizzard that went on for several hours. Mr Pandya and Mr Sen sheltered in one tent. In the other tent Kirkin kept vigil at Uncle Kiran's bedside.

Uncle Kiran was barely conscious. Once or twice he said, 'Ma, Ma.' He also repeatedly mumbled another name, possibly beginning with 'H', which Kirkin could not figure out. This may have been Aunt Anna's Polish nickname. Her parents had immigrated to America from Poland. At about 8 pm Kirkin ran across to the other tent, to inform them that saheb was not breathing. On 19 October 1945, two months before my fifteenth birthday, my loving Phul mama died at the foot of Kanchenjunga, in the lap of the Himalayas he loved so much.

The next morning the two Sherpas appeared with logs of wood for the stretcher. Intrepid people of the Himalayas, they had pulled off what Kirkin had asked of them despite the weather. The blizzard had eased overnight but it was still snowing. The two surviving trekkers and the three Sherpas arranged a makeshift funeral pyre with the logs of wood. As they did so the snow picked up again. Amid a howling wind and blinding snow they placed the body on the makeshift *chita* (pyre) and set it ablaze. Then they immediately commenced their descent. The Sherpas knew that any delay would be fatal; the route down would soon be blocked by freshly fallen snow and they would freeze to death in the wilderness.

Uncle Kiran's remains were recovered the following summer by a team sent from Darjeeling. The team was led by a young Sherpa of Tibetan origin, Tenzing Norgay. The team also recovered the body of the Sherpa accompanying the white man who had planned to set up camp at a point above Green Lake. The Sherpa was sitting on his haunches in a cave formed by ice. His frozen body was completely intact, unlike Uncle Kiran's, which was slightly burnt due to the attempt at cremation. The white man's body was never found; his remains are still lying somewhere in that part of the Himalayas. The peak of Kanchenjunga, silently overlooking the site of the tragedy, was not conquered by climbers till the summer of 1955, two years after Edmund Hillary and Tenzing Norgay scaled the summit of Mount Everest.

DAWN OF FREEDOM

Aunt Anna reached Boston to find that her ailing mother had passed away a few days earlier. A few days after her arrival she received the news of her husband's death. She got on a ship to return to India. It's hard to imagine how she bore that long, lonely journey. Mother and Father wrote her letters, which she received at various ports where the ship docked. She posted letters back from the same ports, which we received in Calcutta.

Just when tragedy struck our family, the freedom movement awakened from its three-year slumber—and with a vengeance.

The catalyst was the return of Indian National Army officers and soldiers to India as prisoners of war. After the war in Asia ended these men were brought from various places in Southeast Asia—Singapore, Rangoon, Kuala Lumpur, etc.—back to their homeland. They were imprisoned in many cities including Delhi, where a prison encampment surrounded by barbed wire was established at the Red Fort. Carried away by hatred of the INA men, former soldiers of the British Indian Army whom they considered traitors, the normally crafty British made a great blunder. As it was, as several tens of thousands of INA personnel arrived in India in batches the INA story, carefully suppressed by the British propaganda machine during the war, gradually became known to the Indian public. As mass trials of so many men would be difficult, the British then decided to put three INA officers on trial at the Red Fort in

Delhi. Of course, the INA's war cry had been *Chalo Dilli* (Onward to Delhi) and Netaji had promised to raise the national tricolour on the Red Fort after liberation. Our colonial masters compounded the folly by selecting one Hindu, one Muslim and one Sikh officer of the INA for the Red Fort trial.

Once the trial of Shah Nawaz Khan, Prem Kumar Sahgal and Gurbaksh Singh Dhillon began in November 1945, the simmering unrest in the country exploded in rage. The British had fatally misjudged how the Indian people would view the INA. Almost all Indians saw the INA's men as brave patriots and liberation warriors, not as treacherous renegades. The trial on charges of treason—'waging war on the King Emperor'—of three of India's finest sons at the Red Fort focused national attention on the issue of the INA prisoners and outraged the country. Three years after the Quit India uprising was brutally crushed, a mood of mass insurrection gripped the country once again for several months, well into the spring of 1946.

The colonial government's police and military opened fire on huge demonstrations protesting the trial and demanding the

BELOW: *Red Fort Trial: (standing from left to right) INA Officers Shah Nawaz Khan, Gurbaksh Singh Dhillon and Prem Kumar Sahgal (January 1946)*

release of all INA detainees in Bombay, Calcutta and numerous other cities. Hundreds were killed. The INA protests united Indians across religious and political divides. I remember reading newspaper reports of demonstrations in central Calcutta where the Muslim League's green flag emblazoned with the crescent and star flew alongside the Indian National Congress's *charkha*-inscribed tricolour. Even the communists had a re-think of their wartime posture and joined the protests with their red flags inscribed with the hammer and sickle. Under Netaji's inspirational leadership, the Azad Hind (Free India) movement in Southeast Asia became a living symbol of national unity, a cause which drew in men and women of all religious faiths, castes and regions of the Indian subcontinent. In the INA, professional soldiers who went from being mercenaries of colonial power to freedom fighters were joined by impoverished but extremely tough Tamil rubber plantation workers of Malaya who had never seen their land of origin. The bogus distinction between 'martial' and 'non-martial' peoples nurtured by the British dissolved. Likewise, the outpouring of solidarity with the INA prisoners that swept India in the winter of 1945 and spring 1946 united Indians—alas only temporarily.

The leaders could hardly remain unmoved. Gandhi visited INA prison camps and hailed their struggle, and described their absent leader as a 'prince among patriots'. Nehru donned his barrister's robes after decades in a gesture of solidarity with the star-studded legal team defending Dhillon, Sahgal and Shah Nawaz at the Red Fort. A photograph of Sardar Vallabhbhai Patel locked in embrace with Sarat Bose—Netaji's older brother and closest political associate—was frontpaged in the newspapers. Sarat Bose was released from nearly four years of continuous incarceration after the end of the war. After the elections of 1946 he was elected as the Leader of the Congress Party in the Central Assembly in Delhi.

The INA fever gripping the nation touched our lives as well. In Hindustan Park in our south Calcutta neighbourhood girls marched in military formation, me among them. We paraded to '*kadam kadam badhaye ja*,' the catchy marching song of the INA. Our marching instructor was Ajitadi, a student in Calcutta's medical college. Later she was Dr Ajita Chakraborty, a renowned psychiatrist. Our role models were the teenaged girls and young women who had joined the INA's women's force, the Rani of Jhansi Regiment, especially its extremely striking-looking and charismatic commander Captain Lakshmi Swaminathan (Lakshmi Sahgal after her marriage in 1947 to Colonel Prem Sahgal). We were at least teenagers but even little boys took to dressing in INA-style military uniforms and giving the INA salutation '*Jai Hind*' (Victory to India). Children were drawn to Netaji's movement in Southeast Asia in large numbers and the INA had an affiliated *Bal Sena* (Kids' Army) to accommodate them.

In the late 1970s my older son, Sugata, went to the University of Cambridge to do a doctorate in history. His supervisor was Eric Stokes, a leading historian. Eric Stokes served in the British Army during World War II. In 1945 he found himself in Malaya where, as a twenty-one-year-old lieutenant, he was tasked with guarding INA prisoners of war and escorting them back to India. When trucks loaded with INA men entered Kuala Lumpur, Stokes noticed people lining the roads. Then they erupted, chanting slogans hailing the INA and Netaji. It was a rude shock for the young English officer and the Indian soldiers accompanying him, who looked on in amazement. Indeed, the experience of the Free India movement led by Netaji had a huge impact on the political consciousness of the three million-strong Indian diaspora in Southeast Asia. Many leading Indian politicians of Malaysia and Singapore in later decades cut their political teeth as young participants in that movement.

That was only the beginning of the ordeal endured by Stokes and his hapless Indian subordinates. Stokes brought the prisoners by ship to Calcutta, from where they were to be transferred to Delhi by train. The instructions were to avoid passing through major stations as far as possible during daylight hours. Even at dead of night the stations on the Calcutta-Delhi route were swarmed by thousands of people shouting slogans. Crowds bearing garlands stopped the train at every station, big and small, to greet the nation's heroes.

Ever since the Great Revolt of 1857–1858 the British had been careful to segregate the soldiers who served in their Indian armed forces from the general population to the greatest extent possible. This became even more important once mass anti-colonial nationalism developed and spread from the beginning of the twentieth century. In end-1945 and early 1946 mutinies occurred or were attempted at cantonments across the country. Then in February 1946 Indian sailors of the Royal Indian Navy (RIN) rose up in Bombay. They renamed their fleet the Indian National Navy. The naval revolt spread to Karachi, Calcutta and other places and at its height involved 20,000 sailors. It was suppressed harshly but the writing was on the wall for the British Empire in India.

The foundation of British control of India—the loyalty of the Raj's Indian soldiers—had been fatally undermined. At the end of the war Netaji had said, 'The roads to Delhi are many and Delhi remains our goal.' When Netaji's soldiers reached Delhi as prisoners, the nation rose up in their support. It was the death knell of the Raj.

While the nation was in turmoil, an upheaval occurred in our extended family. The cause was Uncle Kiran's sudden death. Shortly after he died it became known that he had made a will giving all his assets, including his substantial shares in the Bengal Lamp company, to his wife. For whatever reason Uncle Kiran's three older brothers, my maternal uncles, did not like this at all. My father, a lawyer, had drawn up the will on Uncle Kiran's instructions. Because of this Father became suspect in their eyes. Father told them that he had drawn up the will in his professional capacity and had had no say whatsoever in its contents. But my maternal uncles were not convinced. At the time the controversy erupted Aunt Anna was on her way back to India from the USA by ship. Father pleaded that the issue be kept in abeyance till she arrived, when everything could be discussed face to face. This advice too fell on deaf ears. The three brothers called a meeting of shareholders to take measures to 'protect' Bengal Lamp. Father then resigned from the company's board of directors, where he had a place as the firm's legal adviser. It was an ugly situation. My widowed maternal grandmother sided with Father against her sons. She moved in with us at Rashbehari Avenue and stayed for quite some time. Her youngest son Bimal was studying in the United States when Uncle Kiran died. Uncle Kiran had taken on the responsibility of funding his studies there as their father Lalit Roy had passed away. Uncle Bimal quit his studies and returned to India, where he too moved in with us at Rashbehari Avenue.

Looking back, I feel it's unfair to blame anyone for the crisis. Uncle Kiran's older brothers too felt insecure after his tragic death. My grandmother and Uncle Bimal moved to a flat close to us after some time, and then they moved into Uncle Kiran's flat on Theatre Road. Family relations mended with time but superficially—the episode left a sour legacy. The biggest fallout was that Aunt Anna decided not to stay on in India and returned permanently to the United States. Her departure was very painful for my grandmother. In a letter she wrote, 'Anna has gone away.' Then, referring to her dead son by his nickname, she wrote, 'I no longer have any trace of him in my life.'

Bengal Lamp, my maternal grandfather's dream venture in swadeshi entrepreneurship in colonial times, shut down in 1989. Its closure was part of the decimation of industry in West Bengal that occurred during the 1980s and 1990s. The bulbs and various other lighting devices and fixtures manufactured by the firm for six decades passed into history. The derelict remains of the plant are still there in Jadavpur on Calcutta's southern outskirts, a sad cenotaph to West Bengal's journey from being an industrial powerhouse of India in the 1950s and 1960s to a necropolis of industry over the subsequent decades. At the time it closed down

Bengal Lamp had almost 500 employees. Some of them still live in the 'colony' in Jadavpur built in the early years to accommodate the workers and their families.

In the summer of 1946 a telegram from Darjeeling arrived at Rashbehari Avenue. Uncle Kiran's body had been recovered from Green Lake by a party led by Tenzing Norgay sent from Darjeeling's Himalayan Mountaineering Institute. Tenzing said that the body would have been recovered in pristine form had Uncle Kiran's fellow climbers not attempted to cremate him. At the same time Tenzing and his colleagues recovered the body of the Sherpa accompanying the white man who had passed through Green Lake a few hours before Uncle Kiran expired in the evening. The Sherpa was found huddled inside a cave formed by ice, his corpse completely intact. The white man's body was not found, probably swept away by an avalanche from the Zemu glacier above Green Lake. His mother waited in vain in Darjeeling for news. Aunt Anna was already at the Balaclava villa in Ghoom when her husband's body was found. Father and Mother left immediately for Darjeeling with Mother's eldest brother, Nripen Roy. Uncle Nripen performed the last rites at the Darjeeling crematorium; Father was present. Aunt Anna kept saying to Mother that she would have preferred her husband to have been left undisturbed in the lap of the Himalayas. I remember her repeating the same thing to me in her apartment in Manhattan in 1959, when Sisir and I visited New York City at the end of our one-and-a-half years' sojourn in Boston. While fussing over my small son and new-born daughter she suddenly said, 'Look at me, a foolish grandmother. I imagine they want only me.' The pain of being rejected by part of her husband's family never left her.

In autumn 1945 I started keeping a daily diary. Leafing through its pages, I am a bit surprised by one thing. The diary of an ordinary Indian girl in her early to middle teens contains hardly anything of a personal nature. Instead it's filled with references to the tumultuous events sweeping India on the eve of Independence. I'm especially excited whenever Gandhiji, Nehru or Sardar Patel visit Calcutta. There are lots of references to Subhas Chandra Bose as well—he was dominating the nation in absentia.

The diary also contains copious notes about books which have caught my imagination. At the top of that list is the biography of Madame Curie—the scientist Marie Sklodowska Curie, who won the Nobel Prize for physics in 1903 and for chemistry in 1911—written by her daughter Eve Curie. Madame Curie was the first woman to be awarded a Nobel. I was fascinated by the narrative of her life before she became famous. She was born in Warsaw in 1867 to parents who were both teachers. At that time most of Poland was part of the Russian Empire and the family suffered because of its Polish nationalist beliefs. The family had modest means and for a long time it was uncertain if she would be able to afford higher education—her dream. Finally in the 1890s she arrived in France and enrolled at the University of Paris, where she later became the first ever woman professor. Her years as a student in Paris were hard, as she had hardly any money. She lived without heating in winter and once collapsed in class from hunger. Marie Curie became my personal heroine.

Jawaharlal Nehru's autobiography was another favourite. I read it from cover to cover. The dedication read, 'To Kamala, who is no more.' Kamala, Nehru's wife, died of tuberculosis in Switzerland in 1936. Nehru recounted his years as a student abroad, then his life after joining the freedom movement under Gandhi's leadership. I was especially fascinated by how he coped with being in the public gaze as a highly sensitive and introverted man. I was also struck by the autobiography's literary merit. Next I took up *The Story of My Experiments with Truth*, Gandhi's account of his life until 1921. This left me considerably less impressed. I could not comprehend the great man's philosophy of life very well.

Still, Gandhi was a big presence in our lives. On 26 December 1945 I turned fifteen. Father asked what I would like for my birthday. I instantly replied, 'A charkha' (the Gandhian spinning wheel). A rather large charkha duly arrived. I took to spinning thread on the wheel every day. My cousin Lebudi gifted me two books in Bengali by Netaji: *Taruner Swapna* (The Dream of Youth) and *Nutaner Sandhane* (In Search of a New Age). I was moved by the power of Netaji's words and wrote down an entire passage in my diary, 'It is true that we have been born in an enslaved land, but we will die in a free country. Come, let us all vow that we will liberate India before we die. And if I cannot see India free in my lifetime I pray that I can sacrifice my life in that mission. The road to freedom is difficult, but it is also the road to immortality.'

More presents came my way as I stood first in the final examinations in the ninth standard. A *patano* older brother—not a relative but an elder sibling-like figure—was a pilot who brought me a pair of *nagra*s (slip-on shoes) embroidered with red *zari* (fine gold thread) from Peshawar. Another patano older brother gave me a calendar for 1946. The calendar had a picture of Captain Lakshmi Swaminathan in INA uniform. She looked incredibly dashing. Madame Curie acquired a competitor for the status of my role model.

As fate would have it, after my marriage to Sisir people like Lakshmi, her husband Prem Sahgal, Gurbaksh Dhillon, Abid Hasan (Netaji's sole Indian companion during his ninety-three-day perilous journey by submarine from Europe to Asia in 1943) and S.A. Ayer (minister for publicity and propaganda in Netaji's Provisional Government of Azad Hind, declared in Singapore in October 1943) became members of my extended family. The bond we shared with them was much deeper than what mere ties of blood can confer. My children grew up with the affection and blessings of these wonderful people.

In 1946 and 1947, India was still a colony craving freedom. Netaji's birthday on 23 January was a day of celebration and commemoration throughout the yet to be divided subcontinent. In Calcutta, we woke on the morning of Netaji's birthday to the sound of music. Prabhat pheris, processions taken out shortly after daybreak, meandered through the streets of our neighbourhood and every other neighbourhood of the city, singing patriotic songs in chorus. As the marchers walked and sang, they were showered with flowers from houses on both sides of the street. I looked out of our windows at the sight—a thick spray of flowers enveloping the marching men, women and children. The roof of every house flew the national tricolour proudly. Just after noon, the purported time of Netaji's birth on 23 January 1897, the neighbourhood reverberated with the sound of conch shells being blown in commemoration of the moment. I hadn't collected flowers in advance so had missed out in the morning but now I made up for it, blowing as hard as I could on a conch shell.

In the late afternoon we went to rallies at Deshapriya Park and Triangular Park, both located on Rashbehari Avenue. There I listened to speeches by the INA veterans Colonel Stracey and Colonel Thimayya. More than forty years later, in the late 1980s, Sisir and I spent time with Colonel Cyril John Stracey at his home in Coonoor, a town in the picturesque Nilgiris hills of Tamil Nadu in south India (coincidentally, my father-in-law, Sarat Chandra Bose, was imprisoned in Coonoor for more than three years during World War II). Like a number of other ex-INA officers, he served as a diplomat in various overseas embassies after Independence.

Cyril John Stracey was Anglo-Indian, a community generally known to be even more loyal to the Raj than many British people. He joined the INA and at the end of the war in August 1945 Netaji entrusted him with the task of building a monument to the INA's war-dead on Singapore's seaface. He completed the job in days and an architecturally distinctive monument with three thick pillars—the middle pillar slightly higher than the flank pillars—came up on the seafront. Replicas of the monument stand in several cities of India today. The pillars represented and were inscribed with the three mottos of the INA: *Ittefaq* (Unity), *Itmad* (Faith) and *Qurbani* (Sacrifice). Very soon after that forces under the command of Lord Louis Mountbatten—who was to shortly preside over India's partition as the Raj's last viceroy—landed in Singapore, the site of the British Empire's most humiliating defeat in early 1942 and the birthplace of the INA. He ordered the immediate demolition of the monument.

The order was carried out by a team of Indian soldiers serving in the British forces who were assigned to the task. As they placed dynamite at the base of the monument, a group of surrendered INA men huddled nearby watched in horror. One of them cursed Mountbatten for dishonouring enemy war-dead and said that one day he would meet the same fate as the demolished memorial.

In August 1979 Mountbatten was holidaying on the north-western coast of Ireland. There he was blown to pieces by a bomb planted on his boat by the Provisional Irish Republican Army (IRA), the Irish militants then fighting the British and their allies in Northern Ireland. Gerry Adams, who later emerged as the top leader of the Irish nationalists in Northern Ireland, had this to say about Mountbatten's assassination in November 1979: 'The IRA gave clear reasons for the execution. I think it is unfortunate that anyone has to be killed, but the furore created by Mountbatten's death showed up the hypocritical attitude of the media establishment. As a member of the [United Kingdom's] House of Lords, Mountbatten was an emotional figure in both British and Irish politics. What the IRA did to him is what Mountbatten had been doing all his life to other people, and with his war record I don't think he could have objected to dying in what was clearly a war situation. He knew the danger involved in coming to this country.'

At another mass meeting in Calcutta I saw and heard Colonel Shaukat Malik and Colonel Habib-ur Rahman of the INA. I never had the pleasure of meeting Shaukat Malik in person. By all accounts a colourful character, he raised the national tricolour at Moirang in Manipur's Imphal valley in April 1944. I never personally met Colonel Habib-ur Rahman either; he was Netaji's only Indian companion when Netaji was fatally injured in the air crash at Taipei on the island of Formosa (Taiwan) on 18 August

1945. But I saw him once more from a distance at a performance of a play based on the *Bal Sena*—the INA's auxiliary kids' brigade—at the Kalika Theatre in Calcutta. I was in the audience with Father. Colonel Habib was in the front row along with Anand Mohan Sahay, one of Netaji's close associates in Southeast Asia, Dilip Kumar Roy, Netaji's childhood friend and a famous musician, and Netaji's older brother, Sarat Chandra Bose. Habib-ur Rahman died in 1978 but in the 1990s Sisir and I met his son Naeem-ur Rahman and daughter-in-law Raveen at their home in Pakistan. Sisir of course had met Colonel Habib in person shortly after the end of World War II.

My first sighting of Nehru was also a thrilling moment because I was such a big fan of his books. My diary entry for 8 December 1945 says that I went to attend a rally at Deshapriya Park near our home. A tall stage had been erected there and decorated with a giant portrait of Netaji. The speakers were Nehru, Patel and Sarat Bose. Sardar Patel formally unveiled the portrait. Nehru spoke in Hindustani. The huge crowd was surprisingly orderly. That was because a contingent of INA men were acting as stewards at the meeting.

The next day, 9 December, I got a chance to see and hear Nehru at closer range. Jadavpur University, which is West Bengal's best institution of higher education today, was then Jadavpur Engineering College. It became a full-fledged university in 1955. Its earlier incarnation in the colonial period had close links with nationalist circles and indeed was established to provide a centre of training free of British influence. Nehru came to the College's convocation ceremony. My second maternal uncle, Suren Roy, was an alumnus of the College and closely associated with its administration. He was also an alumnus of Harvard University, where my grandfather had sent him for post-graduate training. Inspired by the 'commencement' (graduation) ceremonies he had seen at Harvard, he arranged for all the alumni of the College to troop into the venue in a procession, starting with the 'Class of

1911'—the first graduates—and ending with the Class of 1945. Each class contingent was led by an alumnus who held aloft a placard with its year of graduation.

Then the guests of honour arrived in a procession. They were showered with flowers by spectators seated on both sides of the aisle as they entered. Because of the crowd and my short stature I couldn't see the dignitaries well but I spotted a Gandhi cap, assumed it was Nehru and aimed the fistful of flowers I had been given at the cap. As the dignitaries walked past I saw my flowers had landed on Sarat Chandra Bose's cap. Nehru was just beside him, looking rather irritated at the hail of flowers. I must confess feeling a bit disappointed that my flowers had landed on Sarat Bose's cap instead of Nehru's. But perhaps there was an element of destiny involved. Exactly ten years later, on 9 December 1955, I got married to Sarat Bose's son Sisir.

Two days later I saw Mahatma Gandhi. We went to a prayer meeting at his ashram at Sodepur, just north of Calcutta. Gandhiji was sitting in his usual posture, bare-bodied, his chest the colour of copper. There was a rush for his autograph. I submitted my autograph book with five rupees, the fee for a Hindi autograph. An English autograph cost ten rupees. In the melee I got back the autograph book of someone else, a student of Calcutta's St Xavier's College. I was able to retrieve my own later and still have it, with Gandhi's Hindi signature.

I ushered in 1946 quietly, immersed in books. The latest additions to my reading list were biographies of Karl Marx and Lenin. And *Mongpu-te Rabindranath* (Tagore in Mongpu) by the young writer Maitreyi Devi (1914–1989). Mongpu is a secluded mountain village in the Kalimpong subdivision of Darjeeling district. Towards the end of his life Tagore, frail and ill, stayed four times in a bungalow in the village while Maitreyi Devi, a protégé of his, cared for him. This was between 1938 and 1940. Maitreyi Devi was the daughter of Surendranath Dasgupta, a classicist and philosopher, and Himani

Devi, sister of Himanshu Rai, the founder of Bombay Talkies. Known both for her intellect and her looks, in the 1970s Maitreyi Devi produced her magnum opus *Na Hanyate* (It Does Not Die), a novel based on her teenage relationship with Mircea Eliade, a young Romanian scholar—later famous in his own right—who had come to India and put up with her family in Calcutta. I loved *Mongpu-te Rabindranath*, in which I discovered Tagore in a more personal light—Maitreyi Devi was quite close to him.

On 23 January 1946 Netaji's forty-ninth birthday was observed across India with great enthusiasm. In Calcutta a mammoth procession wound its way from Deshapriya Park in the south to Deshbandhu Park in the north. Then major trouble erupted in February, sparked by the INA trial at the Red Fort. The newspaper headline read: 'Barracks resound with gunshots—Military Police-RIN ratings duel.' The naval revolt in Bombay spread to Karachi. In Calcutta police and soldiers deployed in strength to suppress demonstrations. Daily life was disrupted as buses and trams frequently went off the roads. I was in the tenth grade, and the countdown to my matriculation examinations had begun. The tumult in the city and across the country distracted me from concentrating on my studies. Moreover I had just started to learn how to play the *sitar*, the stringed instrument used mainly in Indian classical music and made famous across the world in later years by Pandit Ravi Shankar and other maestros. I was loving my sitar lessons.

Poila Baisakh—the Bengali New Year's Day in mid-April—was a beautiful experience in those days, observed in a traditional way in homes. Nowadays, like so many other things it's become a commercialised and media-fuelled ritual, though I believe it's still celebrated in traditional style in Bangladesh. That Poila Baisakh we watched the sun rise over Calcutta from the roof of 190 Rashbehari Avenue. Chhoto kaka—my youngest paternal uncle, Benode C. Chaudhuri—recited Sanskrit verses in his deep voice as the sun rose. I sang a Tagore song welcoming the New Year: '*Aesho hay*

Baisakh aesho aesho'. Then I bathed, put on a new sari and touched the feet of the elders (*pronam*). Later we all sat down to a simple but delicious lunch.

By mid-1946 it was no longer possible to live a serene life in Calcutta. The demand for Pakistan was growing stronger by the day, and more and more Muslims were joining the bandwagon. The Muslim League escalated its campaign, calling for a day of 'direct action' on 16 August 1946. It was an invitation to violence. Bengal had a Muslim League government headed by Huseyn Shaheed Suhrawardy (1892–1963) and large sections of Bengal's Hindus—a minority at forty-three per cent of the province's population—viewed the government with great suspicion.

On 12 August 1946 I visited the Bengal legislative assembly building—an elegant example of colonial architecture set in lawns in the heart of downtown Calcutta—for the first time in my life. The deputy speaker, Tofazzel Ali, was a friend of Father's and he sent cards for us to attend the session on that day. It turned out that the day's session was earmarked for a debate on the Muslim League's 'direct action' call. Father, Mother and I took our seats in the Speaker's Gallery. It was a riveting experience for a fifteen-year-old. The first thing I noticed was the sartorial contrast between the two sides of the House. The treasury benches were dominated by men with longish beards wearing skullcaps and other forms of Muslim headgear. The opposition benches were full of men dressed in Congress khadi; many wore Gandhi caps. Kamini Dutta, a Congress member, stood up and asked permission to bring an adjournment motion. When this was denied by the speaker he started reading it out anyway. The chamber erupted in commotion—catcalls, hooting, thumping of desks. Members started shouting at each other. The Congress's Bimal Sinha and the League's Shamsul Huda became embroiled in a particularly fiery exchange. Huda called Sinha 'son of a zamindar' (Hindu landowner) and Sinha retaliated by calling Huda '*nawab* saheb' (Muslim landed noble). A little later the two left the chamber arm in arm. As they passed the Speaker's Gallery I heard Huda saying to Sinha in Bengali, 'I hope you are not offended that I called you son of a landlord.' I was most bemused by the antics of these gentlemen.

That day I saw many important figures of Bengal and national politics. One was Kiran Shankar Roy, a senior Congress leader who was close to my future father-in-law, Sarat Chandra Bose. Another was the young communist Jyoti Basu, who would serve as West Bengal's chief minister from 1977 to 2000. Then there was Nellie Sengupta. Born Edith Ellen Gray in Cambridge, England in 1886, she was the widow of Jatindra Mohan (J.M.) Sengupta, a prominent Congress leader of Bengal in the 1920s and early 1930s.

The League's 'direct action day', 16 August, seemed like any other day in our upper middle-class and overwhelmingly Hindu south Calcutta neighbourhood. But in the late afternoon Uncle Benode arrived with the news that after the conclusion of a big League rally on Calcutta's Maidan—the vast grassy expanse in the city centre—elements of the dispersing crowds had started looting shops and stabbing pedestrians in central Calcutta. We climbed on the roof of our four-storey apartment building to get a view of the surroundings. Suddenly there was a commotion on Rashbehari Avenue and a gang of miscreants looted a small grocery shop opposite our building. Criminals were clearly taking advantage of the situation. Within minutes all the other shops on the Avenue downed their shutters. Through the evening and night strange noises wafted up to our third-floor flat—not normal street sounds but the unfamiliar noise of prowling mobs. Word reached us that a nearby shop selling radios had been looted.

From that night Calcutta descended into chaos. An orgy of communal violence that lasted over a week left thousands of people dead. The riots are commonly referred to as the Great Calcutta Killings. Tens if not hundreds of thousands fled or had to be evacuated from riot-torn areas to neighbourhoods dominated by their own community. We were in a relatively safe neighbourhood.

But one morning, as we sat at the table in our dining room after breakfast, we heard a sound like the roar of sea waves. As the roaring noise got closer and louder we rushed to the roof. A lone man, running like a hare, ran on to Rashbehari Avenue from the direction of the lakes, chased by a mob of perhaps two hundred armed with sticks. He ran into the ground floor of the house right opposite our building. A huge fracas ensued. A few men from that house and adjoining houses came out to calm the mob. People in the mob screamed, 'Do you not know what they have been doing in the Park Circus area?' Park Circus is a sprawling area wedged between south and north Calcutta. At that time it was overwhelmingly Muslim; it is still predominantly Muslim. One of our neighbours, a bespectacled professor, tried to persuade the mob that the man they were chasing was not to blame for the atrocities against Hindus in the Park Circus area. An old lady came out on the first-floor balcony of the house opposite and pleaded with folded hands, 'He has taken shelter in our house, please spare him.'

BELOW: *Great Calcutta Killings (1946)*

Watching the scene from the roof, I suddenly turned around and headed for the stairs. Father rushed after me and caught hold of my hand, 'Where are you going?' 'I'm going down,' I replied. 'Those men need to be told they can't do this.' He held my hand tightly at the top of the stairs leading down from the rooftop. Rooted to that spot, I heard the sound of a door being broken down. Then there was a seemingly never-ending 'thud, thud' noise—it must have lasted just a few minutes—as the hunted man was dragged out and beaten to a pulp.

I was furious with Father for stopping me from going down. I was convinced that I could have prevented this from happening had I been allowed to reason with the mob. That evening I came down with high fever. Through the night I tossed and turned on my bed in a semi-unconscious state, muttering in delirium.

In the morning our maid Sahachari whispered in my ear, 'Father told me not to tell you. Another man has been killed. The body is lying on the road.' With weak steps I came to the window and looked down on Rashbehari Avenue. There was no trace whatsoever of life and activity on the normally bustling boulevard. A corpse lay on the tram tracks running along the centre of the Avenue. Suddenly a car appeared, its purring engine breaking the ghostly silence. It stopped by the corpse. A white man got down from the car and covered the mutilated body with a large piece of cloth. Then the car drove off. I learned later that the man was Ian Stephens, the editor of *The Statesman* newspaper. I was aghast that it took a Britisher to bring a modicum of dignity to the corpse of an Indian slaughtered by other Indians.

Just months after solidarity with the Indian National Army united people across religious and political divides, Calcutta was literally torn apart by civil war. Self-defence teams were established by young men across south Calcutta, in our para and adjoining ones. Their command-and-control centres were typically located on the rooftop of a neighbourhood's tallest building. Messages would be relayed from roof to roof. Cyclists travelled between neighbourhoods bringing intelligence of the latest clashes and flashpoints. On the night of 20 August conch shells sounded, a warning signal. Then a shout went up, 'Meghnad Saha's house is under attack.'

Dr Meghnad Saha (1893–1956) was a renowned astrophysicist, a scientific genius. He was also elected to India's first Parliament in 1952 from the Calcutta North-West constituency as a candidate of the Revolutionary Socialist Party (RSP), defeating the Congress candidate by a big margin. Until his death in Delhi from a heart attack he pushed strongly for the rehabilitation of post-1947 refugees from East Bengal—he was born in a village near Dhaka and was educated at Dhaka Collegiate School and Dhaka College before coming to Calcutta. I watched as a column of young men armed with *lathi*s (stout sticks) scampered along Rashbehari Avenue towards his house on Southern Avenue, the long road parallel to Rashbehari Avenue by the lakes (today Southern Avenue is Dr Meghnad Saha Sarani). Curfew was in force so they went in single file along the pavement, keeping as close to the houses as possible. Then a fire engine, its bells ringing, went in the same direction followed by a truck full of soldiers, their rifles cocked and ready. After a while the boys returned using pitch-dark lanes and by-lanes; the soldiers had taken care of the problem.

The mob that had set upon the lone Muslim a few days earlier consisted of non-Bengalis—north Indians of the Yadav caste who kept cows in a settlement by the lakes and supplied milk to the residents. But as the trouble intensified Bengali Hindus were drawn into deadly street battles as well. The streets of Calcutta were littered with bodies; even sewers became clogged with corpses in certain areas. The stench was ghastly and military personnel tasked to retrieve piles of corpses wore surgical masks. There were mass cremations of Hindu dead and mass burials of Muslim dead.

After my marriage Sisir and I shared our memories of Calcutta in August 1946. He had some rather interesting experiences to relate. He used a second-hand American personnel carrier left over from war stocks, converted into an ambulance, to rescue Hindus from 'frontline' areas around Park Circus. The streets there were dangerous, as armed rioters roamed and buildings burned from fires set by arsonists. The vehicle was driven by Sundaram, a former INA soldier who had been a migrant in Rangoon running a small shop there before joining Netaji's army and fighting on the Manipur front. It was the beginning of a lifelong partnership for Sisir and Sundaram, a wiry Tamilian. Sundaram became Sisir's right-hand man in all administrative matters at the Netaji Research Bureau, the museum, archive and research centre Sisir established in 1957 at Calcutta's Netaji Bhawan—the house built on Elgin Road in 1909 by Netaji's father Janakinath Bose. Sundaram was practically a member of our family for over four decades; he died in the late 1990s, just a couple of years before Sisir's death in autumn 2000.

It was a new experience for me to be trapped at home for days on end. It was difficult to guess when the mayhem would subside. With no newspapers, the rumour mill worked overtime. Some rescued people were brought from the Park Circus area and put up in a house to the rear of our building. Their arrival increased the tension and anger running through the neighbourhood. One afternoon my Shaejo kaka—my second paternal uncle, Khirode C. Chaudhuri, the doctor—turned up driving a car flying a large Red Cross flag. Uncle Khirode loved Mother's cooking and would eat whatever she had prepared in the kitchen every time he visited. All the markets were closed so there was no possibility of shopping for food. We were surviving on *kochu shak*—leaves of the taro plant—distributed to all neighbourhood residents by the young volunteer teams. But before Uncle Khirode could sit down to a kochu shak meal word arrived that the house of one of his wife's relatives had come under attack near Park Circus. He rushed off there but in vain. The relative—I think his name was Basanta Kumar Sarkar—was killed.

The communal fury subsided after a week but dusk-to-dawn curfews stayed in place for quite some time after that. Rashbehari

Avenue looked eerie at night. I would stand at our third-floor windows and look down on the dark, deserted boulevard. A couple of stray cows wandered about occasionally, the only sign of life.

Around this time I listened to a broadcast by Lord Wavell, the viceroy of India, on our radio. He announced the names of the ministers in India's interim government. It was hard to believe given what was going on around us that Independence was imminent.

The autumnal Durga Puja celebration arrived. The festive season was the usual time for our annual getaway. The riot-scarred city was limping back to a semblance of normalcy. On the train from Calcutta to our holiday home in Mihijam we got into a compartment where a number of Muslim gentlemen were also travelling. My diary entry reads, 'At first we were in the minority [in the compartment]. After some time parity was reached. By the end of the journey we were the majority.' Not yet sixteen, I had absorbed the terminology used all the time in newspapers and on the radio to describe the Hindu-Muslim problem.

Once in Mihijam, I sensed a change in the place. The tensions and crisis sweeping India had penetrated even the serene Santhal Parganas on the Bengal–Bihar border.

1 October 1946 was *Sasthi*, the sixth day of the ten-day Durga Puja. The festive spirit kicks in properly from this day. But unlike previous years I did not wake in the morning to the sound of *dhak*s (traditional drums) from the nearby club where the local Puja took place. In the evening a group walked through Mihijam, singing. Instead of devotional hymns they were singing patriotic songs. This was punctuated with announcements calling on Hindus and Muslims to make the Puja a joint celebration. This sort of thing was completely new.

The next morning, the day called *Saptami*, I woke to the sound of music. A prabhat pheri (morning procession) traversed Mihijam's paths, once again singing patriotic songs instead of the usual devotional hymns hailing the goddess's advent on earth.

The singing alternated with slogans, 'Jawaharlal Nehru *zindabad*, Rajendrababu *ki jai*' (Long Live Nehru, Victory to Babu Rajendra Prasad—the top Congress leader from Bihar and later the first president of the Republic of India).

Rumours spread that there might be communal clashes on *Vijaya Dashami*, the last day of Durga Puja when idols of the goddess are immersed in rivers. The day passed without incident. A couple of days later we heard that a Congress meeting was going to be held on the club premises. Father and I went on hearing that a 'friend' of Subhas Bose would give a speech. The speaker turned out to be the former Hindi teacher at my school in Calcutta. The Congress tricolour fluttered atop a mast at the club. A crowd quite large by the standards of sleepy, secluded Mihijam had gathered. Slogans rent the air, 'Subhasbabu *ki jai*, Subhasbabu *zinda hai*' (Hail Subhasbabu, Subhasbabu is alive).

During a night soon after I had a disturbing dream. In the dream the hills around Mihijam, known as the Kelehi range, were ablaze. I told my parents in the morning. Mother said, 'It's very bad to have nightmares involving fire.' In the late afternoon the morning's papers arrived by the Toofan Mail train, which passed through Mihijam. The headlines were grim. Horrific communal violence had begun in East Bengal's Noakhali district targeting the Hindu minority there. Mahatma Gandhi rushed to Noakhali to contain the violence. I was relieved that Gandhiji had personally intervened. Little did I know that even he could do little to stop the madness and savagery gradually engulfing India.

Kali Puja arrived. The worship of the fierce female deity Kali happens two to three weeks after the end of Durga Puja and coincides with *Diwali* or *Deepavali*, the Indian festival of lights. It's normally a time of great celebration but in October 1946 an air of depression hung over Mihijam. I decided that I wouldn't decorate our house 'Benubon' with candle-lamps, as I had done on our previous sojourns. Darkness fell, and through the tall saal trees we could see lights flickering—the rows of *pradeep*s (candle-lamps) in neighbouring houses. After a little while our caretaker Gokul took matters into his own hands and Benubon too was bathed in light.

Benubon needed some minor repairs. Our repairman Ismail was contacted, but he failed to turn up. Finally Gokul told us, 'Ismail won't come. He is very scared.' What—scared of us? No, he was too frightened to venture out. The Noakhali killings of Hindus were being 'avenged' through mass killings of Muslims in Bihar. Mahatma Gandhi arrived in Bihar, accompanied by Khan Abdul Ghaffar Khan (1890–1988)—the legendary 'Frontier Gandhi' of the Pathan/Pashtun people on India's north-western border. As in Noakhali, Gandhiji could do little amid the carnage.

Soon even little Mihijam was placed under Section 144—the emergency regulation that prohibits the public assembly of more than five persons. On 25 October 1946 a *hartal* (general shutdown) was observed in solidarity with the Noakhali victims. The movement of trains through Mihijam became more and more erratic. Rumours spread that trains travelling at night were packed with corpses of slaughtered people. We were keen to return to Calcutta and would often go to the station to enquire. It was hard to figure out whether it was safe to travel. Finally we returned to Calcutta in the second week of November.

On arrival at the Howrah terminus across the river from Calcutta we were greeted by another novel sight. Groups of Congress and Muslim League volunteers were meeting the arriving trains to provide assistance to passengers from the respective communities. We politely declined the offer of assistance and made our own way. When we arrived home at Rashbehari Avenue we found that our flat had been burgled during our longer than anticipated absence. Fortunately not too much had been taken.

My matriculation examinations were approaching. So I had to make an effort to concentrate on my studies. At school many of the teachers were expecting me to do well and do the school proud. Their expectations made me very nervous. However, I did well in my school's end-year examinations and stood first in class.

In December Calcutta seemed almost back to normal amid the cheer of Christmas and the New Year. Park Street—Calcutta's prime shopping street in the 'European' part of the city—was gaily decorated as usual. Father took me to the Oxford bookstore on Park Street to buy books. I chose a book of photographs taken by the English photographer Cecil Beaton (1904–1980) and a translation of short stories by the Hindustani writer Munshi Premchand (1880–1936). My sixteenth birthday on 26 December was duly observed with a party at home, the atmosphere a bit more subdued than usual. The tension gripping the nation was mirrored in my own tension at the imminent matriculation examinations.

PARTITION

We had recently met a young man from Kerala, Keshava Menon. In fact, he had become a regular visitor to our flat on Rashbehari Avenue. Keshava had got engaged to my maternal cousin Buludi, the older sister of Kutidi, whose dramatic wedding in our flat—orchestrated by Uncle Kiran—I described towards the end of Chapter 4. Buludi had recently qualified as a doctor. She had chosen the Kerala native from a host of suitors. Because of Buludi's arch-conservative father, the relationship was being kept discreet. Our flat became a place for them to meet regularly.

In those days marriages between people from different—and in this case distant—regions of the country were very rare. So Keshava added a touch of novelty to our lives. I would observe him with curiosity, in the way people today might observe a non-Indian foreigner about to marry into the family. Keshava would eat Bengali cuisine—*machher jhol* (fish curry) and rice—with relish. We would be invited to his rented flat to eat Kerala cuisine. My plate would be covered with a huge *papadom*—I had never seen such a size before. Under the papadom were neatly arranged bowls with *rasam*, *sambhar*, etc. It was my first taste of the cuisine of southern India, and possibly my parents' as well. At the end there would invariably be a bowl of *payasam*—vermicelli pudding. I noticed that the south Indian version was nowhere near as thick as Bengal's *payesh*. It was almost a liquid and was best consumed by sips rather than with a spoon.

Keshava Menon was a political activist, a member of the Congress Socialist Party. The CSP was formed in 1934 by left-wing Congressmen as a caucus and pressure-group within the fold of the Indian National Congress. These left-leaning leaders had become dissatisfied by the mid-1930s with the conservatism on a range of matters of Gandhi and many of his closest colleagues. Keshava and Father would discuss politics a lot over the meals, and I would listen with great interest. Keshava was particularly close to Ram Manohar Lohia (1910–1967), the socialist leader known to be a stormy petrel of the independence struggle. He told us that Lohia was going to visit Calcutta soon and he would bring Lohia to our home. I was very excited.

ABOVE: *Keshava Menon and Krishna's cousin Buludi after their marriage, Calcutta (1948)*

On 23 January 1947 Netaji's fiftieth birthday was celebrated on a huge scale all over the country. In the evening it was as if Diwali, the festival of lights, had moved to January. Houses across Calcutta were decorated with candle-lamps in commemoration of the absent leader. Many INA officers—all household names—came to the city to participate in the celebrations. They were mobbed wherever they went, especially by young people.

Meanwhile the instability gripping the nation caused instability in my life as well. The matriculation examinations kept getting postponed. On 20 February 1947 I heard Clement Attlee, the British prime minister, announce on the radio that Britain would leave India by 30 June 1948. This was a reasonable timetable for departure. Lord Mountbatten, who had replaced Wavell as India's viceroy on 12 February, later advanced the date to August 1947.

Around this time Lohia came to dinner at our flat with Keshava Menon. He took a quick glance around our living room. It had

ABOVE: *Krishna's father Charu C. Chaudhuri playing the sitar at Rashbehari Avenue, Calcutta (late 1940s)*

no less than five musical instruments: organ, sitar, esraj, tabla, harmonium. Then he said, 'There is music in the house.' Lohia spoke English well but he preferred to converse in Hindi. He was already a known advocate of *angrezi hatao* (throw out English) and the adoption of Hindi as the national language of independent India. This led to an argument with Father. Father said he agreed fully with *angrez hatao* (throw out the English) but could not see why their language and literature had to be banished as well.

At the dinner table Lohia suddenly looked at me and asked, 'Are you a communist?' I was somewhat taken aback and did not know what to say. Father came to my rescue, 'She's sixteen, she hasn't made up her mind yet.' Lohia locked his eyes with mine and said, 'If you want to become a Muslim Leaguer, even that is tolerable. But whatever you do, don't ever become a communist.' Lohia detested the Indian communists. And he was surely aware that it was something of a fad at that time among some educated young people to become communists, on paper at least. I think he regarded the Indian communists as anti-national elements whose loyalty lay with foreign powers rather than with the Indian people. He must have been particularly outraged by the Communist Party of India's (CPI) active collaboration with the British regime against nationalist patriots during and after the Quit India uprisings. Lohia was an underground activist during the war and was caught only in May 1944. He was taken to the Lahore Fort, a notorious prison where my husband Sisir was also held in solitary confinement around the same time. Sisir was almost skeletally thin when he was released from a medium-security prison in Lyallpur (now Faisalabad in Pakistan) in September 1945, but perhaps because of his youth his health more or less recovered with time. Lohia's health never really recovered.

Before leaving Lohia signed my autograph book—in Hindi, of course. He teased me that he wouldn't give me an autograph because I hadn't divulged my political leanings, but gracefully relented. It was a rare opportunity to meet Ram Manohar Lohia, whose ideas would be so important over many decades after Independence in shaping the politics of northern India, especially in his native Uttar Pradesh.

Keshava and Buludi's wedding is etched in my mind for a particular reason. The wedding was held at the felicitiously named Cosmopolitan Club on Ballygunge Circular Road in south Calcutta. The civil registration ceremony complete, the guests had just sat down to enjoy tea and an assortment of snacks when shocking news rippled through the gathering: Mahatma Gandhi had been shot dead in Delhi. It was 30 January 1948. Many of the *bor jatri*s (the bridegroom's guests) were Congress socialists like Keshava himself. The plates of food remained uneaten as they got up and left. These were men opposed to many aspects of Gandhi's politics but the death by assassination of the man Netaji had hailed as the 'Father of Our Nation' in a radio broadcast in 1944 was a hammer blow to nearly all Indians. We too returned home in a state of shock. As I entered our Rashbehari Avenue apartment the radio was on and I could hear the haunting lyrics of one of Tagore's melancholy songs.

My matriculation examinations were again postponed, to start from 19 May instead of 17 April. It was difficult to predict what might happen next. When I received my admit card on 8 May, it seemed that the examinations would finally be held. I finished my examinations on 7 June 1947. To celebrate my school friends and I went to the cinema. We saw a movie that starred Bharati Devi (1922–2011) in the female lead. She was a well-known actor in Bengali cinema for many decades, almost till her last years. At that time she lived next to us on Rashbehari Avenue. We would often see her relaxing on an adjacent rooftop from the windows of our flat.

By that time it had been decided that India would be partitioned. On 3 June a radio broadcast by Mountbatten announcing the Partition of India was aired from London and New Delhi. This caused great worry to my family. Mother had relatives in Dhaka while Father had relatives in Mymensingh. Both these districts would definitely go to Pakistan.

Much later I learned that my future father-in-law Sarat Chandra Bose had made a valiant last-ditch attempt to prevent the partition of Bengal by putting forward a proposal in May 1947 for a 'United Bengal' based on mutual recognition, equality and power-sharing between the elites of the province's Muslim and Hindu communities (Muslims were then a narrow majority in Bengal, fifty-four per cent, and Hindus a very large minority at forty-three per cent). The proposal's co-author and co-signatory was Abul Hashim, the secretary of the Bengal Muslim League. They negotiated—mostly in 1 Woodburn Park, Sarat's residence—for four months between January and May 1947. The proposal recommended the immediate dissolution of the communal Muslim League ministry of Bengal and its replacement by a broad-based transitional coalition government. The British took the proposal seriously enough for Mountbatten to record two variants of his broadcast on 28 May 1947. The alternative version, which was not broadcast, said that 'Bengal was one of the Provinces for which Partition was demanded, but the newly formed Coalition Government of Bengal have asked for their case to be reconsidered.' Sarat Bose showed enormous vision but the proposal perhaps came too late to save Bengal from being divided now that the British departure was scheduled for August 1947 rather than June 1948. My husband Sisir Kumar Bose has written a detailed account of the making and provisions of the United Bengal plan in his biography of Sarat, *Remembering My Father*. The biography was published at the time of Sarat Bose's birth centenary in 1989 and released in a new edition from Delhi in 2014, on the occasion of his 125th birth anniversary.

Father's two sisters were both in East Bengal at their respective *shoshur bari*s (in-laws' residences). Uncle Nirad, who had moved to Delhi during the war after taking a job at the headquarters of All India Radio, sent a directive that they should stay put. This was completely unrealistic advice. My *chhoto pishima* (youngest paternal aunt), Sarojbala, had four daughters and felt particularly insecure about them. Her postcards to Mother became increasingly desperate in tone. Mother replied trying to calm her down. Mother wrote to her that if necessary we would all subsist together on dal and rice. As refugees Aunt Sarojbala and her family did face a difficult life in West Bengal after Partition. But she always told me that Mother's kind words had given her some peace of mind because already the uprooted (*udbastu*s) from the east were being viewed as a liability in the west, even among relatives.

Bengal's Hindus overwhelmingly supported Partition because they were fearful that Jinnah and company might swallow the whole of Bengal. In that event the situation of Hindus as a minority would become dire. Most Bengal Muslims rejoiced at the formation of Pakistan including sixty-three per cent of Bengal's land area—the loss of the rest of Bengal to India seemed bearable. They realised their historic mistake soon enough, starting in the early to mid 1950s. That's another story. At that time the mood on the streets of Calcutta was just as Sadat Hasan Manto, famous for his searing writings on the Partition, described a slum in Bombay. Half the slum dwellers raised the tricolour and burst crackers. The other half raised the green flag and also burst crackers.

On 20 June 1947 I wrote in my diary, 'Bengal has been divided.' On that day Bengal's legislative assembly met, first as one and then separately in two groups of 'members elected from the Muslim-majority districts' and 'members elected from the rest of the Province'. In the joint session ninety members voted for the existing constituent assembly (i.e., India) and 126 for the new constituent assembly (i.e., Pakistan). The vote was almost entirely on communal lines, except for four low-caste Hindu members who voted with the League (there were also a few abstentions). The leader of this autonomous scheduled-caste tendency in Bengal, Jogendra Nath Mandal, moved to Karachi as Pakistan's first minister of labour, law and justice. He was a follower of Dr Bhimrao (B.R.) Ambedkar, one of the architects of the Republic of India's constitution proclaimed on 26 January 1950. Mandal realised within a few years that he had been taken for a ride, resigned in October 1950 and came back to India, where he died in 1968. His resignation letter sent to Liaquat Ali Khan, Pakistan's prime minister, on 8 October 1950 is a devastating indictment of the top Muslim League leadership and of the very nature of Pakistan as a sovereign state.

As a family we were terribly demoralised by the division of Bengal. Although long-time Calcuttans, Father and Mother were both from East Bengal and had grown up there. It was a wrenching personal blow for them. My diary entry for 20 June records an evening discussion at our flat above Rashbehari Avenue between Mother, Father, my Chhoto kaka (Uncle Benode, the youngest of Father's five brothers) and me. We were all very sad. Father kept saying that after all the sacrifices and contributions Bengal and Bengalis had made to the cause of India's freedom this outcome was hard to accept.

Uncle Nirad wrote to Father that I should be sent to Delhi for a vacation since I was sitting at home after the conclusion of my examinations. I couldn't travel alone so Mother accompanied me. Mother and I reached Delhi on 30 July 1947. We stayed until 15 September. For one-and-a-half months I had a ringside view of Independence and Partition in the national capital. It was a truly extraordinary experience.

Our address during those weeks was the P&O Building on Nicholson Road in old Delhi. Uncle Nirad lived with his family in a flat in this building. The road was named after John Nicholson (1822–1857), a particularly brutal military officer of the East India Company. He led the re-capture of Delhi from the rebel sepoys in

September 1857, and died days later of wounds from the fighting. After his death he became a central figure in the British narrative of 1857. An impressive statue of Nicholson in uniform, a very long sword dangling from his waist, stood on a pedestal at Nicholson Park off the road. After Independence it was removed to Northern Ireland, his place of origin, where it stands today in the grounds of the school he went to as a boy.

At that time Uncle Nirad was writing the book that would make him the internationally known writer Nirad C. Chaudhuri a few years later—*The Autobiography of an Unknown Indian* (1951). I would wake early in the morning to the 'clack clack' of his typewriter. Delhi was having a typically hot summer and most of the building's residents would sleep on the roof at night. Because I had a tendency to catch cold easily I would sleep on the flat's south-facing verandah on a rope charpoy (*khatia*). Late into the night Uncle Nirad would sit on the floor beside my bed, reading out long passages from the manuscript. There was a lot about his childhood in East Bengal—tales of the ancestral village of Banagram, stories of life at the turn of the century in Kishoregunj town. My father, two years older than Uncle Nirad, featured very frequently in the narrative. After a while I realised that I was Father's proxy in these reading sessions. 'Tell dada this is how I've written about Kishoregunj,' Uncle Nirad would instruct me, 'and remember to tell dada how I've described the Durga Puja in the village.' One day he whispered the title of the book in my ear. 'Tell dada, but no one else must know,' he said.

The reading sessions were fine but I would get uncomfortable when Uncle Nirad launched into one of his diatribes about India and its future (or rather, the

BELOW: *Nirad C. Chaudhuri at work on* The Autobiography of an Unknown Indian, *Delhi (1947)*

lack of a future). A fervent, almost comical loyalist of the British Empire, he was convinced that India had no future whatsoever after British rule. He told me that India would split into many fragments once the British left. The concept of dialogue was unknown to Uncle Nirad throughout his long life (he died aged 101 in 1999 in Oxford, having permanently moved to England in the 1960s). He would simply deliver monologues on a variety of subjects. I was the ultimate captive audience but would occasionally protest. He was adamant that while some individual Indians would certainly shine in the world, India as a country had no prospects. I was especially disturbed by how disrespectfully he spoke about our national leaders. Gandhi was a crafty, scheming operator, a prize hypocrite of *bania* (commercial) roots. Nehru was an opportunist par excellence. As for Subhas Bose, he was a political novice. Uncle Nirad grudgingly acknowledged, however, that Bose had a certain courage of conviction and a willingness to sacrifice himself in his misguided cause.

One day the sound of the typewriter woke me up just before daybreak. Seeing me awake Uncle Nirad stopped typing. 'Come, let me introduce you to the stars,' he said. Standing on the dark verandah on Nicholson Road, we watched the stars twinkling in the sky above Delhi and he explained various things about the galaxy to me. I actually knew quite a bit about astronomy already, from lessons with Father while gazing at the sky in Mihijam.

The sun rose and Mother and Aunt Amiya, Uncle Nirad's wife, busied themselves preparing breakfast. By then Uncle Nirad had moved on from astronomy to a discourse on philosophy. At the breakfast table he started talking about nineteenth-century English literature. He was highly pleased to hear that I had already read all of Jane Austen's novels as well as the works of the Bronte sisters, Charlotte and Emily. Then he started on Western classical music. Here I couldn't keep up any more; I had been raised on Rabindra sangeet and lately also understood Indian classical music and its *raga*s. I had brought a small sitar along to keep up the practice. By the time we finished breakfast my head was spinning from this avalanche of information about so many different subjects.

Uncle Nirad worked at All India Radio (AIR). He went off to his office for a couple of hours and was back by lunchtime. Post lunch, he had more plans for my education. 'Come, let me introduce you to Plato,' he said, plucking a thick, heavy tome from his crowded bookshelves.

ABOVE: *Krishna practising the sitar in Delhi (1947). Her cousin Kirti is with her*

My education at Nicholson Road extended to more practical things. On Uncle Nirad's instructions his two older sons, my cousins Dhruva and Kirti, started to teach me to ride the cycle. I was a quick learner and after falling over a few times in Nicholson Park I soon mastered the art of cycling. Then Dhruva, Kirti and I started to cycle around Delhi, a pleasant experience in 1947 when Delhi was an uncongested city ideal for cycling. Our other preoccupation was photography. Dhruva and Kirti have both been excellent photographers throughout their adult lives. At that time Dhruva—who is two years younger than me—was starting to learn photography with a box camera. Uncle Nirad, who was greatly into Dutch painting, would ask me to strike poses imitating the girls and young women in famous paintings by Dutch artists. I enjoyed it I have to say.

BELOW: *Krishna cycling in Delhi (1947)*

For a few days in the first half of August we had a guest, the daughter of a friend of Uncle Nirad's. Her name was Zubaida and she was visiting from Lucknow. She was a little older than me, and Dhruva, Kirti and I called her Zubaida *baji* (older sister). She was sweet and we got on well. One evening a few

Photographic Show

Saturday, July 23, 1949

EXHIBITORS:

Miss Krishna Chowdhuri
Dhruva Chowdhuri
Kirti Chowdhuri
Prithvi Chowdhuri
Sanat Majumder
Sarit Majumder
Benode C. Chowdhuri

ALSO COLLECTION OF PHOTOGRAPHS BY

K. C. Chowdhuri, and
Charu C. Chowdhuri

SLIDES FROM COLOURED PHOTOGRAPH BY

K. C. Chowdhuri

Miss Krishna Chowdhuri
presents her compliments
and requests the pleasure of
Mr. Sunity Kumar Chatterji's presence
at a PHOTOGRAPHIC SHOW
at 190/c, Rashbehari Avenue, Top floor,
on Saturday, the 23rd July, 1949.

Photographic Show : 3 to 7 p.m.
Lantern Slide Show of
Coloured Photographs : 7 p.m.

ABOVE: *List of exhibitors of the Photographic Show (1949)*

RIGHT: *Invitation letter for Photographic Show at home at 190C Rashbehari Avenue (1949)*

Muslim colleagues of Uncle Nirad's at AIR came for a farewell dinner. As government employees they had opted to go to Pakistan and were leaving shortly.

As Independence Day approached my mood became downbeat. I was sure Uncle Nirad would not let me take part in the celebrations to mark the passing of the Raj. I started to miss Calcutta. There I would have joined the prabhat pheri on the morning of the 15th, singing as we walked. Uncle Benode wrote to me from Calcutta promising to send the Independence Day issue of *Anandabazar Patrika*—the staunchly nationalist Bengali newspaper. It was small consolation.

A couple of days before the 15th Uncle Nirad noticed my downbeat mood. He said, 'All right, if you want to join in the mafficking you are free to do so. I won't stop you.' I was elated.

A Goanese family, the Pintos, lived in the adjoining flat. The woman's name was Gladys Pinto. At midnight on 14-15 August I listened to Nehru's 'tryst with destiny' speech on the radio in Auntie Gladys's flat. In the morning I joined the throngs celebrating on Delhi's streets. I remember it was very dusty. The hundreds of thousands of people out on the streets were kicking up the dust. Mountbatten passed by in a horse-drawn carriage. Then the Union Jack was lowered and the tricolour raised in its place. Amid the jostling I suddenly realised that I was about to be trampled by a policeman mounted on a horse. Someone pulled me out of the way just in time.

Dusk fell. Dhruva, Kirti and I were still on the streets. Delhi was blazing with light. All the major public buildings and historic monuments had been lit up for the occasion. As the evening progressed the streets gradually emptied. Suddenly Kirti started to recite Tagore's poem on the end of the reign of the Mughal emperor Shah Jahan, 'You have departed, O monarch… Your kingdom gone, like a dream… Your throne vanished…'

To those born after Independence it is hard to convey what that day meant to us, those born and raised in an enslaved country.

Delhi went from celebration to carnage in a matter of days. Hindu and Sikh refugees from western Punjab had been trickling into Delhi for months. Now the influx became a flood. The apartment building on Nicholson Road overlooked one part of the boundary walls of the Red Fort. Refugees camped by and even on the wall. A Sikh family lived in a flat on the ground floor of the building. One day the Sikh gentleman returned in a severely injured condition. He had got into a tonga—the horse-drawn taxis of Delhi in those days. The Muslim tonga driver plunged a knife into his abdomen and fled. He pulled out the knife, took off his turban and bandaged his stomach with the cloth. He then drove the tonga home. He died after three days.

Soon Delhi was put under curfew. The longest spell lasted eighty-four hours, three-and-a-half days. We would go on the roof of the P&O building to try and get a sense of what was going on. The city was covered with thick plumes of smoke from numerous fires. There was a tin of egg powder at home. I don't recall ever seeing this product again; possibly it was a leftover from wartime rations. Mother and Aunt Amiya used it creatively and a variety of egg dishes appeared at the dining table. Uncle Nirad decreed that the atmosphere in the flat must remain as normal as possible. To that end he banned the use of certain words from our conversations: murder, looting, rape.

At the beginning of the riots I had a hair-raising experience. The household's domestic help Dhonu did not return home at night from the All India Radio offices, where he had gone on an errand. Early the next morning Dhruva, Kirti and I got on our cycles and set off towards New Delhi to look for him. The streets were really deserted but because it was an early hour we thought nothing of it. My sari was rising up above my ankles in a mild breeze as I cycled. Kirti, all of twelve, said crossly, 'Didi, mind your sari. People are looking at you.' Who could be looking at me? I had been concentrating hard on managing the cycle but now I looked around and upwards. People clustered at windows and on balconies were staring down at us. As we approached an intersection we saw a group of khaki-clad soldiers in front of us. We coolly cycled past them. Then we heard a shrill whistle; they were asking us to stop. We dismounted and they approached us. 'Where are you going?' they asked. 'All India Radio,' we replied. They looked at us in disbelief. 'Are you mad? Do you not know what's going on all over the city? We had to open fire at this intersection just a little while ago. Leave this area immediately.'

We panicked. I had never thought I could cycle so fast. We had no idea what direction we were going, we just went. After a while I was overcome with exhaustion and fear. I stopped, got off and sat down by the road. Dhruva managed to find a *tongawallah* (tonga driver). We got on the tonga with our cycles and reached home via a circuitous route. By that time the morning papers had arrived and Mother, Uncle Nirad and his wife were on the verandah, looking out for us with anxious faces. To this day it surprises me how Uncle Nirad could have sent the three of us—a girl of sixteen and two boys aged fourteen and twelve—out to find his missing servant, apparently oblivious to the tinderbox situation in Delhi.

One day the curfew was relaxed for half an hour. Dhruva went out to the post office and came back with a sheaf of letters. There were several from Father. Both he and Uncle Benode were very worried at the news from Delhi. One letter contained news of my matriculation results. I had not done very well but had passed in the first division with seventy per cent marks. Father wanted me to return to Calcutta as soon as possible to be enrolled in college.

That was easier said than done. The rioting had subsided but Delhi was far from normal. During the rioting Dilip kaka—Dilip Sanyal, a professor of English at Delhi University's Ramjas College and a friend of Uncle Nirad's—had joined us in the flat on Nicholson Road. Eventually it was decided that he, Mother and I would travel to Calcutta together. On 15 September 1947 the three of us boarded a train at Old Delhi station. The station and its vicinity were littered with putrefying corpses. Uncle Nirad came to see us off. He kept saying that it would have been better to wait for a few more days before travelling. For once he was right.

That train journey from Delhi to Calcutta is one of the unforgettable experiences of my life. A group of Sikhs were travelling in our compartment. A young Sikh girl about my age was sitting on the bench opposite mine. On the way out of Delhi the train got on the bridge over the Yamuna river. The shallow waters on both sides were strewn with corpses. Suddenly the girl said to me excitedly, '*Dekho dekho, kaisa khoon*' (Look, look at the blood). She had spotted the body of a small child that was still oozing blood. I closed my eyes. A bit later she told me that she was the only survivor from her family. Everybody else—male and female, young and old—had been killed in a massacre in West Punjab's Lahore district. She had some distant relatives in Calcutta's Sikh community so was travelling there.

The train to Calcutta continued its journey and after some time I resumed looking out of the window. Soon I noticed something odd. Pieces of luggage were being thrown out of other compartments. How strange. Then I realised that the bundle-like objects were not pieces of luggage but human beings. A gang of men were roaming through the train, looking for Muslims. Whether they were killing those they found and then throwing them out or throwing them out alive I do not know. They soon appeared in our compartment—five or six men including two Sikhs. Once they learned we were from Bengal they became very interested in us. They seemed convinced that we were Muslim because most of Bengal was now part of Pakistan. A sharp argument broke out between the gang and our Sikh co-passengers. The orphaned girl led the confrontation with the gang. The argument was in Punjabi but I could make out some of it. She gestured towards Dilip Uncle and I heard her say, 'He's a professor.' Then she gestured towards Mother and me, saying that we were from an aristocratic family. The gang was not persuaded but they moved on to the next compartment with an ominous 'We're coming back.'

A little later the train pulled into Kanpur. Evening had fallen. I looked out on to the platform and saw a large contingent of British soldiers—'Tommies' as they were known then—lined up in formation, guns at the ready. They boarded the train and moved systematically through the carriages. The gang was apprehended and taken away. I had never imagined that the appearance of British soldiers could provide such deliverance. We had been an independent country for a month at that time.

After Kanpur there was no further disturbance. I climbed on an upper bunk and lay down, but could not sleep. Through the night the train tore across the plains of north India towards Calcutta—no longer the capital of Bengal but the capital of 'West Bengal', a new entity covering just over one-third of the territory of undivided Bengal and containing a similar proportion of the population of the pre-partition province.

Father received us at the Howrah terminus the next day. He was shocked at how pale and haggard I looked. He said, 'I thought I sent you to Delhi for a vacation.'

IN AN INDEPENDENT COUNTRY

My higher education commenced in newly independent India. Suddenly I felt rather grown-up. Early in the morning I would catch the tram from the stop in front of our building on Rashbehari Avenue. The tram would already be packed with girls heading to Ashutosh College in Bhowanipur, another area in south Calcutta. During the journey the tram would be like a bird sanctuary, alive with the chirping chatter of dozens of teenaged girls. I was a student of Intermediate Arts (IA); those in the science stream were studying towards the ISc. After the two-year Intermediate

RIGHT: *Traffic in Calcutta in the late 1940s*

programme it took another two years to earn a bachelor's degree with honours. A master's degree took another two years. At that time the Intermediate programme of Ashutosh College had a good reputation. Every year a number of its students would be ranked among the 'top twenty' in the Intermediate examinations.

On my return from Delhi I found that Father had got me admitted to another established institution of the city, the Gokhale Memorial Girls' College. This too was in the Bhowanipur area, a bit further from our home than Ashutosh College. The reason was that the institution—named after Gopal Krishna Gokhale (1866–1915), the social reformer and political leader from Maharashtra—had its own buses to take students from home to college and back. So I would not have to suffer Calcutta's public transport. Father's protective instinct was understandable but the college bus proved to be a problem rather than a godsend. I would sit in it for hours while it dropped off students at addresses across Calcutta. After a week I rebelled. This was untypical given my diffident temperament but apart from the monotony of travelling around the city for no reason my friends from Ballygunge Girls' School—including Kumkum, my closest friend—were all enrolled in Ashutosh College. Father saw reason and agreed.

I felt a bit overwhelmed by the college environment. Hundreds of chattering girls streamed up and down the staircase as classes began and ended. Shy and quiet by nature, I couldn't mingle easily. One day Kumkum told me that some of the girls were discussing my aloofness. They thought I was stand-offish and put it down to intellectual snobbery. I was stunned. Far from harbouring feelings of superiority, I had no idea that people might be interested in talking to me. From then on I made it a point to go up to my fellow students and exchange pleasantries.

The classes were very crowded. Typically each lecture had more than one hundred students. I soon noticed that the students referred to the teachers by their initials, such as 'A.V.', 'B.G.', 'M.M.' and so on. This practice endures in Calcutta and West Bengal to this day—I do not know about elsewhere in India. I found it odd then and still do. On the other hand, the students were reduced to faceless creatures known by their identifying numbers, almost like the inmates of a gulag. Thus I was 'roll number 369'.

The impersonal, indeed anonymous nature of the process of teaching and learning bothered me. It seemed to border on dehumanisation, of teachers and students alike. A few years later my disquiet at the whole experience led me to write an article on the subject. In the article I severely criticised the mechanistic nature of teaching and learning I had encountered, especially the absence of any human connection between the teacher and the taught, who were treated like a mass of cattle. I sent the article by post to *The Statesman*, the English daily of Calcutta. To my surprise it was published, under the pseudonym I had used: 'Roll Number 13'. To my even greater surprise, the issues regarding the education system raised in the article touched off an animated discussion. For several months the newspaper's 'letters to the editor' featured missives on the subject. That was the first published piece of my life.

I was unimpressed by most of the teachers I had at the Intermediate level. 'B.G.' would gesticulate dramatically while teaching the poetry of Alfred Tennyson. 'S.C.' taught us civics. Every few minutes he would pause and ask, 'Do you understand?' Faced with silence, he would then say, 'You do not understand. You will never understand.' 'M.S.' was a handsome man and the girls drooled over him.

Suddenly one day there was an exception. The teacher was a little late to class and the girls were chattering away. No one noticed him enter. Then a deep voice came from the direction of the teacher's platform, 'As befits members of an assembly, I expect decorous behaviour from you.' The room fell silent. He started taking the class—in economics. The lecturer with such unusual gravitas was very young—in fact he was just twenty-three years old at the time. I had noticed him once or twice before in the corridors of the college. He had a disability and walked with a limp.

I soon became a fan of Amlan Datta (1924–2010), who would go on to have a stellar career for decades afterwards as a professor of economics as well as a social and political commentator. He would relate his lectures to everyday concerns. One day he said, 'Why did the fish in the market this morning cost three-and-a-half rupees per *shaer* rather than three rupees, or four rupees?' (The *shaer*, a traditional unit of measurement and weightage, gradually became obsolete after India adopted the metric system in the early 1960s.) He then proceeded to explain a basic of microeconomics—how price is determined by supply and demand—with exemplary clarity.

Admiring the young lecturer's pedagogy from a distance, I never thought any person-to-person connection was possible. But he surprised me there as well. Towards the end of my two years of Intermediate studies, I had gone to college to find out when the results of our preparatory tests for the Intermediate examinations would be released. I ran into him on the stairs. He stopped and said, 'You are Krishna, right?' I nodded. He said, 'You have done very well in the preparatory tests, except in Bengali to some extent. As for the economics paper, you would have done even better if you had written the introduction to your answer to the second question a little differently, and if you had elaborated the conclusion of your answer to the fifth question a little more.'

In the Intermediate examinations my best performance was in economics, well over eighty per cent. At that point I was sure I would study economics honours for my bachelor's degree. That didn't happen but decades later I had the chance to meet Professor Amlan Datta many times. He came to speak at Netaji Bhawan in Calcutta, and I often found myself as his co-speaker at various public events and conferences in the city.

Apart from the languages, English and Bengali, Intermediate Arts students had to take three compulsory subjects. A fourth subject was optional. Most students took an optional subject because it made sense to do so. The marks in the optional subject in excess of thirty (the pass mark) were added to the candidate's total marks from the other five papers. Thus strong students were able to augment their already high marks, while average students who would otherwise get a second division stood a chance of squeezing into the first division. Students normally chose an optional subject that was known to yield high marks.

Father was into learning for its own sake, and a devotee of the liberal model of education. He decided that I would take anthropology as my fourth subject. He was very interested in anthropology, a modern, exciting discipline that had only recently appeared in the world of Western scholarship. He had read some of the pioneering works in the field and wanted me to partake in his excitement. There was just one problem—anthropology was not offered in my college. Moreover, it was taught in only one institution in the whole of south Calcutta, the Science College on Ballygunge Circular Road. So I started going there to study my fourth subject. I remember I learned to measure human skulls. It was rather lonely because I was the only student. And it was difficult to fit in trips to the Science College alongside my studies at Ashutosh College. Khitish Prasad Chattopadhyay, the principal of Science College, had been a contemporary of Subhas Bose as students at Cambridge decades earlier. He was strict about attendance. After some time even Father realised the impracticality of the arrangement and my fourth subject was discontinued. By that time it was too late to enrol in a different subject. When the results of the IA examinations were published I found my name in the top twenty, in the eighteenth position. Had I had an optional subject I would have easily made it into the top ten.

The independence of India coincided with another major change in our lives. Father quit practising as a lawyer. The reasons were several and mutually reinforcing. Father and some of his brothers had chosen law, medicine and engineering in part because they were professions that could be pursued independently, without necessarily being employed by the colonial government or a British company. But Father was basically a man of the arts and letters, and he never really enjoyed practising law. Moreover most of his clients were from East Bengal and Partition cut them off. And he had already quit as the Bengal Lamp firm's legal adviser during the conflict after Uncle Kiran's death.

Above: *Charu C. Chaudhuri, Krishna's father (late 1940s)*

Meanwhile jobs were available in the newly formed government of West Bengal. Father first joined the health department of the new government as a legal expert. His office was in the Writers' Building, the iconic red building dating to the late eighteenth century located in the heart of Calcutta's downtown area. The headquarters of Bengal's colonial administration for a long time, it was now the central secretariat of the West Bengal government. During British rule it overlooked Dalhousie Square, named after Lord Dalhousie, governor-general of India from 1848 to 1856. Dalhousie's predatory policies did much to bring on the Great Revolt of 1857–1858. After Independence Dalhousie Square was renamed B.B.D. Bagh in honour of Benoy, Badal and Dinesh, three Bengali revolutionaries who conducted a daredevil suicide raid on the building in December 1930. The Writers' Building is presently undergoing the biggest renovation in its history and Chief Minister Mamata Banerjee and some of her colleagues are temporarily based in a modern building in Howrah, just across the Hooghly river from Kolkata.

At Writers' Building Father wrote public health laws and regulations, including an anti-smoking bill which must have been among the first—if not the first—of its kind in the world. Soon his skills got noticed and he was appointed as a secretary of the West Bengal Legislative Assembly (Vidhan Sabha in Bengali and

Hindi). He held this job for about twelve years, from 1948 till his retirement in 1960. Throughout that period he was the actual author of the Speaker's rulings on various matters.

I became a frequent visitor to the Vidhan Sabha and thus had a ringside view of the politics of West Bengal during the first decade after Independence. The Vidhan Sabha building is a graceful, low-slung structure set in lawns just down the road from Writers' Building and opposite Raj Bhavan, the official residence of the governor of West Bengal. At that time it was relatively new; as the plaque by the main doorway notes the seat of what became the West Bengal legislature after 1947 was inaugurated in 1931 by Francis Stanley Jackson, Bengal's British governor. Jackson was Bengal's governor from 1927 to 1932. A former chairman of Britain's Conservative Party—the 'Tories'—he had been the captain of England's Test cricket team in his youth. Jackson had a fairly explosive sending-off from his posting to Bengal. In February 1932 he narrowly escaped an assassination attempt at the convocation ceremony of Calcutta University. The revolutionary who opened fire on him with a pistol was Bina Das, a twenty-year-old student. She was the daughter of Beni Madhab Das (1866–1952), a famous educationist who was the young Subhas Chandra Bose's teacher at Cuttack's Ravenshaw Collegiate School at the end of the first decade of the twentieth century. A staunch patriot, he was a very important early influence on Netaji's life. Bina Das (1911–1986) was imprisoned until 1939; then she was in jail again from 1942 to 1945 after joining the Quit India uprising in 1942. I had the privilege of meeting Binadi in 1971, when she led relief operations from Calcutta's Netaji Bhawan for the flood of refugees entering West Bengal during the Bangladesh liberation war.

Father really enjoyed his job at the Vidhan Sabha, and not just the routine work. He supervised the flower show held every winter in the assembly building's sprawling gardens. He was also the man behind the initiative to decorate the building's lobby and corridors with paintings of Bengal's iconic figures. The idea first entered Father's head as a way of supporting a few of his artist friends—including Atul Bose, the noted portrait painter who lived on Bondel Road close to our flat on Rashbehari Avenue. At that time even well-known artists often struggled to make ends meet. Father realised that commissioning works for the legislative assembly building would be a neat way of helping Atul Bose and others. He approached Bidhan Chandra Roy, the chief minister. Dr Roy was very positive and asked Father to go ahead and float a tender. The contract would be awarded to whichever artist put in the lowest bid! Dr Roy, West Bengal's chief minister from 1948 till his death in 1962, had many strengths—he was a renowned physician in addition to being a politician—but he was not exactly a man of culture. Father suppressed the file for a few weeks. Once the chief minister had forgotten about the matter the artwork began to be commissioned, sans tender. The first oil paintings to be put up in the Vidhan Sabha building were of Subhas Chandra Bose and Rabindranath Tagore, both done by Atul Bose. Many others followed, done by different artists. All the works adorn the West Bengal Legislative Assembly to this day.

ABOVE: *Krishna's father Charu C. Chaudhuri in his study at Rashbehari Avenue, Calcutta (late 1940s)*

When the assembly was in session Father would often return home very late. One day he returned late even though the assembly was not in session. Chuckling, he said, 'I had to make sleeping arrangements for Jyotibabu.' The communist legislator Jyoti Basu—later West Bengal's chief minister from 1977 to 2000—had decided to take shelter on the assembly premises to evade an arrest warrant because members could not be arrested from inside the assembly compound. Father organised a bed, bed linen and a mosquito net for him. Jyotibabu took up residence in a room in the building and stayed there for a few weeks. One day he tried to sneak out to his party's office and the police caught him.

Jyoti Basu remembered Father and his kindnesses decades later. In 1996 I found myself on the same plane with him from Kolkata to Delhi. He was West Bengal's chief minister and I was a Member of Parliament, serving the first of my three terms in the Lok Sabha. Father had passed away in 1987. When our conversation touched on him Jyotibabu said in English, 'He was a very learned man.' Indeed, Father had a special interest in constitutions and constitutional law; his personal library at Rashbehari Avenue had lots of books on the making and meaning of constitutions. His expertise in this area was very useful in his role at the assembly. Whenever a constitutional issue arose government ministers and journalists alike would seek out his opinion. Father would write the Speaker's rulings in a very balanced, even-handed way.

On another occasion—the date was 20 February 1950—Father returned later than usual. He said, 'Saratbabu is going to speak in the assembly tomorrow. He's not well and wants to speak while seated. The chamber only has standing mikes, so I had to arrange for a mike he can use.' Sarat Chandra Bose—Netaji's older brother and my future husband Sisir's father—had been elected to the West Bengal legislative assembly just a few months earlier in 1949 in a by-election for the South Calcutta constituency. He contested as an opposition candidate against the Congress's nominee. Sarat Bose was not present in Calcutta during the election campaign—on medical advice he was resting in Switzerland. Even without campaigning he won by a huge margin. Father was among the tens of thousands who voted enthusiastically for him. Sisir was then in England taking advanced medical training in London and Sheffield, and received the news of his father's massive by-election victory by cable from Calcutta.

The morning papers on 21 February 1950 brought us the news that Sarat Bose had died the previous night of a heart attack.

In London, Sisir was leaving his lodgings in Hampstead for the day's work at the children's hospital on Great Ormond Street when he received the news. 'The calling bell and the telephone rang simultaneously,' he has written in his biography of Sarat, *Remembering My Father*. The cable from Calcutta arrived just as an Indian journalist based in London telephoned. Sisir picked up *The Times*, which was lying on the doorstep, to find that the London newspaper had an obituary of his father.

Until December 1955, when I got married to Sisir and moved into the mansion at 1 Woodburn Park built by Sarat Bose in 1927, I visited the Vidhan Sabha frequently (after my marriage I went once in a while). I was such a regular fixture there that someone jokingly called me 'the princess of assembly house'. The smartly uniformed orderlies all knew me and would intone gravely when I turned up, '*Didimoni* [star sister] has come.' I would sit in the Speaker's Gallery and watch the proceedings. I remember Ishwardas Jalan and Saila Mukherjee in the Speaker's chair. Bidhan Roy's tall figure contrasted with his singular lack of speaking ability. He could never complete a sentence, whether in English or Bengali.

The opposition benches, dominated by communists and socialists, were limited in numbers but not in punch. Jyoti Basu often launched scathing attacks on the government. The leftist opposition was even more active on the streets. They would call hartals (general strikes) at the drop of a hat; in 1953 they set buses and trams ablaze across Calcutta to protest a slight increase in fares. One day leftist agitators *gherao*-d (surrounded) the assembly complex. I wanted to go home but was trapped by the siege. Jyotish Joardar, an anti-colonial revolutionary fighter who was a close associate of Subhas and Sarat Bose in the freedom struggle was then an opposition MLA (Member of the Legislative Assembly). He came to my rescue and managed to get me out through one of the gates.

One day I was drenched by a sudden rain shower while walking to the assembly building after getting off at the nearest tram-stop.

Ballalbabu, the house marshal, lived on the premises. His wife came to my rescue on that occasion and I returned home wearing one of her saris.

Looking back, I feel that I gained my first lessons in the politics of India's democracy from those visits to the West Bengal Legislative Assembly so many decades ago.

After I passed my Intermediate examinations, a big family debate ensued over what I should study for my bachelor's degree and also which college I should attend. Uncle Nirad wrote from Delhi that I should study history honours. Thick volumes about the ancient Greeks and Romans arrived by post from the capital. I wanted to study economics honours. Father and Uncle Nirad both pooh-poohed that; according to them economics was not a serious subject. Amid the uncertainty, Father suggested Sanskrit Honours. I knew Sanskrit reasonably well and liked it. But the case for devoting my higher education to the ancient language was far from clear to me.

Finally English Honours was selected as a compromise. I was very disappointed not to be able to read economics honours. But I had to accept what my guardians decided.

Then the issue of which college I should go to came up. Unlike today, there wasn't a frenzied scramble for seats so the choice was pretty open. At that time Presidency College was established as far and away the leading college of Calcutta. It was the first choice for almost all meritorious students. I applied to Presidency. Within a few days a white postcard arrived—I had been accepted. Then a discussion began about how I would travel from Rashbehari Avenue in south Calcutta to Presidency's campus on College Street in north Calcutta. The public transport available was poor, limited to a fleet of rather old buses run by a few Punjabi families. So studying at Presidency was considered infeasible. It was a great pity. Just a couple of years later I joined the MA programme in English at Calcutta University, whose main campus is next to Presidency's. Some of my MA classes were taught by Presidency faculty. By then the transport issue was resolved; brand new, blue double-decker buses had been introduced on north-south routes at the initiative of Bidhan Roy's government. I would get on in front of our apartment building on Rashbehari Avenue and get off on College Street.

A few of my friends enrolled at Lady Brabourne College, Calcutta's premier college for young women. Located at Park Circus, it was easily accessible from south Calcutta. But for whatever reason this option was not considered. Loreto College, another top women's college located on Middleton Row off the Park Street thoroughfare, did come up as a possibility. By then the deadline for submitting applications there had passed. Still Father took me there one day. A strict-looking European nun in white told us we were too late. As we were leaving, she called us back and asked to see my Intermediate marksheet. She glanced at it and said, 'Come back tomorrow with the entrance fee. And here are the forms you need to fill out.'

It's still something of a mystery to me why I was not allowed to study at either Presidency or Loreto. In the latter case, there was no transport issue. Two years later, after sitting my BA examinations, I took up learning French at Calcutta's Alliance Francaise. This was located on Park Street and I commuted there easily by tram from Rashbehari Avenue.

So I stayed on for my BA in English Honours at Ashutosh College, where academic standards were mediocre. There were a few good professors—'M.M.' (Mohinimohan Mukherjee), 'J.N.C.' (Jitendranath Chakravarty), and 'S.C.' (Sujata Choudhury) among the women. But it was still a mass production line for graduates and there was almost no individual interaction between the faculty and the students. It was this experience that led me to write the critique of the state of higher education that was published in *The Statesman* under the pseudonym 'Roll Number 13'; I wrote it just after sitting my BA examinations. My fellow students were also an uninspiring bunch—the students of high calibre had all gone to Presidency, Lady Brabourne or Loreto. I felt unmotivated in this atmosphere. To make things worse, there would occasionally be strikes at college, called by leftist student organisations opposed to the Congress government. The main gate would be picketed and lecturers prevented from entering. The intrusion of politics into institutions of higher education—which would destroy higher education in West Bengal over subsequent decades—had begun. Another oddity was the overly strict segregation of female and male students. Our classes were in the morning and the boys' classes in

RIGHT: *Krishna (1950)*

the afternoon. The boys were allowed to enter the college only after we had exited.

My outlet during my BA years was music. Tarapada Chakraborty home tutored me twice a week in Indian classical music. He was a hard taskmaster. I was his favourite student but he scolded me constantly for not doing *rewaaz*—singing practice—two hours in the morning and two hours in the evening. He didn't realise the demands on my time. I was simultaneously taking sitar lessons at the Bengal Music College. I progressed well and soon my playing reached the 'intermediate' stage. Bengal Music College was an affiliate of the Lucknow Music College and Pandit Ratan Jhankar came down from Lucknow to take my intermediate examination. I passed comfortably and the pressure increased even more as the final examination—for the *sangeet visharad* title—approached. The preparations involved rewaaz at home two evenings a week accompanied by a percussionist—a *tabalchi* or tabla player.

The day after my BA examinations ended Mother and I travelled by plane to my favourite holiday destination—Darjeeling. That Calcutta–Darjeeling flight was my first experience of flying. Father was already in Darjeeling. Some of the Vidhan Sabha's committee meetings were being held in Darjeeling—at the town's Raj Bhavan, until Independence the summer retreat of the British governors of Bengal. Dr Bidhan Roy was present along with a number of his cabinet ministers. Ministers in those days were not remote from the public. The members of the cabinet would stroll freely around Darjeeling's Mall. One, Jadav Panja, was given to not wearing shoes and would walk barefoot even in Darjeeling's cool weather. I noticed how cold his feet were when we ran into him one day and I bent down to touch his feet. The journalists covering the meetings in Darjeeling referred to him as 'barefoot babu'.

We stayed close to Raj Bhavan, at a lovely two-storeyed house a little below the north side of the Mall. It was called 'Holmden'. The house faced Kanchenjunga, with magnificent views from all the rooms, even the bathrooms. A chora bato or shortcut ran from the house to Raj Bhavan. Father took the shortcut to work and back. His *chaprasi* (orderly) Sudhir, who had travelled with him from Calcutta, followed him carrying files, resplendent in a red uniform decorated with gold thread.

I have very nice memories of the people of Darjeeling. A kanchi (young girl) would bring me morning tea in bed. On the tray, beside the crockery, would be letters that had arrived the previous afternoon. I would ask her why she didn't give me the letters the previous evening, once the post arrived. She would break into a smile, her reddish cheeks glowing as she did. This was the way the British did things in the old days, her parents and grandparents had told her. She found Sudhir's reaction to the mountain climate quite comical. It was May and hardly cold by Himalayan standards. Sudhir would often disappear and she would say, '*Woh palang mein giya*'—He has gone to bed, curled up under a woollen blanket of course.

Darjeeling of course provided a great setting to indulge my interest in photography. That year I took a lot of portraits of local girls and women. I used to buy fruits every day from a very pretty girl in the market—she belonged to the Lepcha community, one of the indigenous peoples of the eastern Himalayas. She was always smiling. One day I pointed my camera at her and she started screaming. It turned out that according to the beliefs of her community human beings whose images were taken became cursed and died. She did relent after a few days. There were other experiences with the women in the market. Mother was buying *batabi lebu*—pomelo, the largest citrus fruit. She took one in her hand and asked the seller—a woman from the Bhutia community, who are of Tibetan origin—whether the inside was red or not. As I clicked their photograph, the woman grinned from ear to ear and said, '*Ami to bhitore poshi nai*' (I haven't been inside, you know).

Two years later we were in Darjeeling again, and during that visit I had a truly memorable experience. The date was 29 May 1953.

As you get on the Mall from the Hill Cart Road, the famous café Keventer's is on the left. We would often sit on its open roof and have coffee, a scene re-created by the actors Ranbir Kapoor and Ileana D'Cruz in the 2012 Bollywood movie *Barfi!*, which is set mostly in Darjeeling as it was decades ago. Just a few steps from Keventer's is Glenary's, the equally famous patisserie. Opposite Glenary's is Frank Ross, a pharmacy as well as a general convenience store (a 'drugstore' in American English). Father and I were standing in front of Frank Ross when a commotion broke out. Not some unseemly disturbance, just a commotion. A young man was running with a newspaper and shouting, 'Everest conquered!'

Because of my family's interest in the Himalayas and in mountaineering, I had grown up on stories of the exploits and tragedies of climbing expeditions. Father's library had quite a few books on failed attempts to conquer Mount Everest—the world's highest peak at 8,848 metres or 29,029 feet above sea level—and I had read them all. I was especially fascinated by the story of the English climbers George Mallory and Sandy Irvine, who disappeared in 1924 while assaulting the summit. They were last seen in the late afternoon of 8 June 1924 as two black dots on the snow a few hundred metres short of the summit by a colleague who was positioned at a slightly lower altitude. The great mystery of Mallory and Irvine revolves around whether they did succeed in making it to the summit and died during the descent. Most authoritative analyses, especially those published in the last few decades, conclude that they died during the final climb towards the summit, although what precisely happened to cause their death is the Himalayas' eternal secret.

I knew that Irvine's ice-axe had been found in 1933 at an altitude of 27,760 feet. Of the bodies of the missing climbers there was no sign—until May 1999, when Mallory's remains were discovered at about 27,000 feet. He had almost certainly fallen to that spot from a higher altitude. Nestled for seventy-five years below the summit, Mallory's frozen body was somewhat damaged but clearly identifiable from name-tags on the clothing: 'G. Leigh Mallory'. Mallory was one of the top climbers of his era; he died ten days before his thirty-eighth birthday. Irvine, a relative rookie in high-altitude climbing, was just twenty-two years old. His body has not yet been found. At the same time as Mallory's remains were discovered an used oxygen cylinder dating to 1924 was recovered from 27,820 feet, which means that Mallory and Irvine had reached at least this altitude and most probably beyond. How much beyond, we will never know for sure.

It was incredibly thrilling to be in Darjeeling the day Everest was conquered by India's Tenzing Norgay and New Zealand's Edmund Hillary. We already knew Tenzing—he was the man who had brought Uncle Kiran's body back from Green Lake below Kanchenjunga to Darjeeling in 1946. Father and I almost ran to Tenzing's home. He lived in the Alubari bustee (slum) in the town, by the Calcutta Road. The slum was squalid but Tenzing's modest home was neat and clean. We sat in the living room with his wife and two daughters. I snapped a few photos of the women of the Everest conqueror's family, dressed in the traditional clothes of the mountain people. Father and I, aged twenty-two, were the first to reach their home to congratulate them.

BELOW: *Tenzing Norgay with Krishna's father in Darjeeling (summer of 1946)*

One of the perks of Father's job was travel to other parts of India, mostly for the annual conferences of the Speakers of the Vidhan Sabhas. Mother and I would tag along when we could. These trips gave me the opportunity to return to Delhi, see Bombay, and explore Srinagar and the Kashmir Valley.

In Bombay we stayed close to the Gateway of India, in a street to the rear of the Taj Mahal Hotel. I was struck by how different the sea-face was from the beach of Puri, which I had seen as a child. In Puri huge waves crashed down on sandy beaches. In Bombay there was none of that. The calm waters of the Arabian Sea stretched to the horizon. Occasionally the sea got a little agitated and mild waves landed on the wall of the embankment. The impact produced a shower of water drops on my head, like a divine blessing.

Delhi was already familiar territory. So after the end of the meetings there Father, Mother and I took a trip to Agra, Mathura and Vrindavan. I had seen many pictures of the Taj Mahal but realised they were no substitute for experiencing the real thing. It's a marvel one can visit over and over again and be entranced every time. After seeing and touring the Taj during the day we took a tonga to see it by night, in the moonlight. It was an ethereal vision. I remember how quiet and empty it was there at night; in fact Mother was a little scared. At the Agra Fort I was most impressed by the white marble structures built by Shah Jahan in the seventeenth century inside the red sandstone fortress constructed by his grandfather Akbar. At Fatehpur Sikri, the sixteenth-century city founded by Akbar a short distance from Agra, I remember the red stone buildings and of course the enormously imposing Buland Darwaza, the gateway to the site.

Mathura and Vrindavan were disappointments in comparison. There was none of the spiritual atmosphere I had expected from their celebrated status in Hindu texts, mythology and music and from reading one of the compositions—*Brajangana Kavya*—of the remarkable nineteenth-century Bengali poet Michael Madhusudan Dutt (1824–1873), the 'Byron of Bengal'. The infestation of touts near the temples was particularly appalling. The only relief was a visit to the Ramakrishna Mission's local ashram. There the atmosphere was serene, the garden full of flowers. Suddenly the sky became overcast with dark clouds. I stepped on the bank of the Yamuna river under stormy skies and briefly felt the essence of Vrindavan as it should have been, and perhaps was some time in the distant past.

The Speakers' Conference in Srinagar in spring 1954 was the occasion of my first visit to Kashmir (I visited again in 1976 for a family holiday and then in 2003 leading a group of parliamentarians). The atmosphere at the conference was relaxed and friendly and I was invited to all the lunches and dinners. In fact, wielding my Rolleicord camera, I emerged as the event's *de facto* official photographer. One day lunch was at one of the palaces of the former Dogra rulers of the princely state of Jammu and Kashmir (J&K). I heard Dr Bidhan Roy was looking for me. I found him in the palace's gardens with Saila Mukherjee, the speaker of the West Bengal legislative assembly, and a few others. One of the others was Bakshi Ghulam Mohammad, then the prime minister of J&K (the 'chief minister' title in use in all other Indian states was introduced later in J&K). And there was a beautiful young couple—Karan Singh, scion of the Dogra dynasty and J&K's titular head of state, with his wife. Dr Roy asked me to take a group photograph. I focused and pressed the shutter; it didn't respond. I tried again and realised the shutter wasn't working. But the group thought I had taken two pictures and I was too embarrassed to tell them otherwise. They said 'thank you' in unison and dispersed.

There was nothing much wrong with the camera—the man at a camera-shop on Dal Lake fixed the jammed shutter in a few minutes. But I was sorry to lose the opportunity to take such an interesting photograph. Later I met Karan Singh many times. He came to speak at Netaji Bhawan in Calcutta in the 1980s. More recently we spent many years together in Parliament: I in the Lok Sabha and he in the upper house, the Rajya Sabha. He was a member of the parliamentary standing committee on external affairs which I chaired from 1999 to 2004 and we met often. And I often remembered our first meeting in Srinagar in 1954, when we were both twenty-three years old.

Unknown to me, Kashmir had just seen a major upheaval. In August 1953 Sheikh Abdullah had been dismissed as J&K's prime minister and arrested in a plot orchestrated from New Delhi by

Nehru's government. He spent most of the next twenty-two years in prison. The order for his dismissal and arrest had been issued by Karan Singh, the titular head of state (*sadr-e-riyasat*). Bakshi Ghulam Mohammad, Sheikh Abdullah's deputy and a key player in the plot, had then taken over as prime minister. Mass protests across the Kashmir Valley had been suppressed with violence and dozens had been killed in police firing. Hundreds of pro-Abdullah activists were in jail. I was not aware of any of this at the time. But I do remember that during a *shikara* trip on the Dal Lake—the shikara is the distinctive boat of the waterways of Kashmir—the boatman sang Sheikh Abdullah's praises and bitterly criticised Bakshi Ghulam Mohammad. He reflected the sentiment of the masses, among whom the deposed and jailed Sheikh was a figure of worship.

Blissfully unaware of the turmoil, we were engrossed in taking in the natural beauty of Kashmir. As soon as the conference ended we set out to explore the Valley. Father, Mother and I travelled to Pahalgam, the scenic resort south of Srinagar. Saila Mukherjee and his wife were with us. There tents were pitched by the fast-flowing and rock-strewn Lidder river, in a meadow overlooked by snow-capped mountains. We had three tents: a large one for sleeping, a medium one for cooking and a small one for toilet needs. Sailababu's kitchen tent was always busy. We were constantly walking in the area and mostly ate at the local roadside eateries. They served delicious meals of *roti*, *tarka dal*, mutton and chicken.

Then we decided to travel to Amarnath, where the cave-shrine of Lord Shiva is located. This is quite an arduous journey along mountain paths and tracks. It takes about five days from Pahalgam to Amarnath, where the holy cave is situated at an altitude of 12,756 feet, nearly 4,000 metres above sea level. Shanti Kabir, wife of the scholar and politician Humayun Kabir, joined us for the trip. I had fond memories of the Kabirs and of playing with their children Pasha and Leila from childhood vacations in Darjeeling, when we stayed at Uncle Kiran's 'Balaclava' house in Ghoom and they put up nearby.

ABOVE: *Krishna and her parents vacationing in Pahalgam, Kashmir (1954)*

Horses and supplies were organised and we set out. The first night-halt was at Chandanwari, where we stopped at the dak bungalow. It was a steep climb from Chandanwari to Sheshnag the next day. A narrow path hugged the mountains on one side while a deep ravine fell away on the other. I felt nervous riding on such a sheer path. I got off my horse and started walking. The *ghorawallah* (horse-supplier) accompanying us said to me that it was safer to ride; the horses knew exactly how to negotiate this terrain. I looked up once and saw he was right—the horse carrying Mother was going up a semi-vertical stretch with total confidence. We came to a stream, with a wooden bridge across it. The horse carrying Mother stopped at the bridge and tested it by knocking on the wood with its front hooves. Then it went down into the stream and carried Mother through the water to the other side. The smart horse had judged that the bridge might not be able to bear the weight of my tall, well-built mother.

When we reached Sheshnag at an altitude of 11,780 feet (3,590 metres), we found a desolate field of snow and ice. The place's feature is its lake in which *sheshnag*, the king of serpents, is said to reside. But where was the lake? It was very much there, just covered with a thick sheet of ice. Father struck the layer of ice hard a few times with his walking stick and it broke like glass, revealing water beneath. The lake, which always freezes over in winter, is fed by melted snow and by streams coming down from the surrounding mountain-tops. Its water drains out through the stream we had just crossed and joins the Lidder at Pahalgam, about 4,500 feet below Sheshnag. There was a tiny bungalow on the frozen meadow by the lake, overlooked by towering snowy peaks. It had just two rooms; we packed into one of the two rooms for the night. Mother and Shanti Auntie sang devotional songs till late into the night.

The next morning we learned that the track to Amarnath was still not open. It was blocked by snow and ice and would not open for another week. We had covered about seventeen miles from Pahalgam and were about twelve miles short of the Amarnath cave. We mounted our horses to return. My horse refused to turn around—it was determined to continue towards Amarnath! It had to be coaxed and cajoled to return. From Chandanwari the route was easier and I part-cantered and part-galloped till our tent camp by the Lidder. Saila Mukherjee and others were sitting on deckchairs having late-afternoon tea when we arrived.

I felt a certain spiritual connection to Pahalgam. Premananda Tirthaswami, a monk of East Bengal origins known to my family, had spent decades meditating in the mountains of Kashmir, especially around Pahalgam. We met him after he returned to West Bengal around the time the raiders from Pakistan invaded the Kashmir Valley in October 1947. By then he was elderly. He spent the last dozen years of his life travelling between Calcutta, Darjeeling, Puri, Benares, Agra and Patna. But he had a considerable following of disciples in the Valley. One such family, the Wattals, had us over to their house on the Airport Road in Srinagar. They were Kashmiri Pandits, related to Jawaharlal Nehru's family. There we met another distinguished-looking elderly gentleman. I don't remember his name but I think he was a high official in the administration of Hari Singh, the last Dogra king of Jammu and Kashmir. When we stepped out in Srinagar with him I noticed that the people on the streets were very respectful to him.

The place that enchanted me the most during that 1954 visit to Kashmir was Sonamarg. Sonamarg (literally 'Golden Meadow') is an alpine valley fifty-five miles north-east of Srinagar, close to the Zojila Pass that connects the Kashmir Valley to Ladakh. It is at an altitude of 9,200 feet (2,800 metres), perched below some major glaciers. The place is snowed under for nearly half the year. When we went there the surrounding peaks were still draped in snow. I was taking photos with my Rolleicord when a few Indian Army personnel appeared and asked me not to take pictures. Then, as now sixty years later, Sonamarg was an important base and transit point for the Indian Army. Indeed the soldiers are the only inhabitants of Sonamarg during the winter months.

On the return journey to Srinagar we got stuck. A large convoy of army vehicles was in front of our car. One of the military trucks broke down and keeled over, stalling traffic in both directions. We waited by the road with a young army officer. He wore glasses and had a very intelligent look about him. He kept assuring us that a crane would soon arrive and remove the broken-down truck.

A few days after we returned to Calcutta, Father showed me a small report published on an inside page of *The Statesman* newspaper. He said, 'Isn't this the officer we met near Sonamarg?' Indeed it was. He had been killed in a firing incident on the Ceasefire Line in Kashmir, as the Line of Control was known then.

AT UNIVERSITY

The trip to Kashmir in 1954 was just after my MA examinations. My two years as a MA student at Calcutta University in the early 1950s carry many wonderful memories.

After I finished my BA examinations, there was a lengthy hiatus till the results came out. I decided to put the time to some constructive use and enrolled at Calcutta's French cultural centre, the Alliance Francaise, to learn French. My first teacher there was Mademoiselle Bossenec. She was a stickler for correct pronunciation.

LEFT: *Krishna with her parents in the sitting room at the Rashbehari Avenue flat (early 1950s)*

I made a great start to learning French with her. Then I had Madame De Sarkar, a Frenchwoman married to a Bengali. Aunt Neelima, my doctor uncle Khirode C. Chaudhuri's wife, told me, 'Why are you learning French? Learn Hindi, it will come to some use.' But I liked the language so much, I kept up the French classes on the side even during my rather hectic MA studies. At that time there was a lot of interest in the French language and culture among young people of my generation in Calcutta. Youngsters would sometimes greet each other with '*comment allez-vous*?' instead of '*kaemon aachho*' (how are you) in Bengali. The response was easy enough: '*Tres bien, merci!*' (very well, thanks).

ABOVE: *Krishna in the Rashbehari Avenue flat's living room (1953)*

The French classes had boys and girls my age, but also much older students. It was nice to be in the company of a diverse crowd. I travelled from Rashbehari Avenue to the Alliance Francaise on Park Street by tram, a very pleasant way to make the journey. Today Calcutta's trams are an endangered form of public transport. This is a great pity. I wish we could learn from how tram lines built well over a century ago continue to be a key part of mass transit in so many twenty-first-century cities in Europe and even beyond, Istanbul for example. I remember how the breeze would waft through the windows as the tram trundled along, blowing my hair and the aanchal of my silk sari askew. That breeze was to me the harbinger of freedom, of adulthood.

Among my fellow students in the advanced French class was Lady Ranu Mookerjee, one of the most cultured and sophisticated women of Calcutta. Lady Ranu (1907–2000), a strikingly beautiful woman, was married to Sir Biren Mookerjee (1899–1982), a pioneer of the steel industry in India. Her father, a Bengali, had been a professor of philosophy at the Benares Hindu University (BHU). Ranu—her nickname, her formal name was Preeti—became acquainted with Rabindranath Tagore early in her life and was known, accurately or not, as the poet-laureate's 'muse' in his later years. Despite the age gap we got on very well, and it was the beginning of a friendship which would last a lifetime. At that point I was just embarking on a freelance career as an art critic after devouring books on modern art in Father's library; on that more below. Lady Ranu was prominent in the arts scene of Calcutta—she was a patron of the city's Academy of Fine Arts. I would run into her at art exhibitions, and she would start talking to me in French. I was not so comfortable in conversational French but would do my best to respond.

ABOVE: *Krishna after her graduation (early 1950s)*

Sometimes I would go straight from French classes on Park Street to attend classes for my MA in English at Calcutta University's College Street campus. I'd often arrive a little late and out of breath. As I stepped into Professor Priya Ranjan Sen's classroom I would hear him calling out my roll number (7) as he took attendance. 'Present, sir,' I would pant as I scuttled in. He would reply jovially, 'Yes, sir, I have seen you, sir.'

A professor of English at Calcutta University, Professor Guha, lived opposite us on Rashbehari Avenue. When I started my MA studies, he said to Mother, 'Why are you sending her to do an MA? There aren't too many girls who do an MA. Just the ones who are not married. Your daughter is pretty, she won't have trouble getting married.'

The good professor changed his mind soon. Some time later he told Mother that the girls in the new batch of MA English students were exceptionally bright.

Indeed, we were quite a girl gang. Kajal Bose and I often took the lead in organising activities. Later, as Kajal Sengupta, she was a popular professor of English at Presidency College and was one of the first women on the college's faculty. Ushashie, Nandita and Rani were among the other girls. We organised a reading of *Murder in the Cathedral*, T.S. Eliot's verse drama on the assassination of the archbishop in Canterbury Cathedral in 1170. We also enacted some scenes from Shakespeare's *Macbeth*, with Kajal and myself playing witches. Our professors were the main audience.

Next we performed a play, *Everybody Comes to Mabel*. It was a light comedy. This was performed in the hall of the University's Ashutosh Building. Kajal played the role of Mabel, and I was the 'other woman'. At the end of the play I eloped with Mabel's husband. The show was quite successful and the then governor of West Bengal, Haren Mukherjee, invited us to perform the play in the Raj Bhavan's marble hall. I remember the hall was packed. Nowadays all this might seem rather ordinary, but back in 1952 it was unusual for young women to be in the public eye in this way.

I enrolled at Presidency College, where some of my classes were taught. Presidency's campus is next to the main Calcutta University campus on Calcutta's College Street. I remember the fees at Presidency were seventeen rupees a month. There I had the opportunity to study with Tarak Nath Sen, a legendary professor of English. Another distinguished professor was Subodh Chandra Sengupta; he was strict but gentle at the same time. In the English department's seminar room on the first floor Professor Amal Bhattacharya taught us modern poetry.

My classmates at Presidency included three wonderful and bright young men: Arun Kumar Dasgupta, Binod Kishore Ray Chaudhury and Dhriti Kanta Lahiri Chaudhury. Arun—later, as 'A.K.D.G.', a respected professor of English at Calcutta University and Presidency College—was a somewhat serious and reserved sort. But the other two—Dhriti and Benu (Binod Kishore)—were a riot. Because the trio and I were always seen together, we became known as 'Goldilocks and her Three Bears'! Benu's older sister Rani was the fifth member of our close-knit group. Rani was drop-dead gorgeous, and she retains her classy elegance to this day. Unfortunately for the legions of young men interested in her, she was already married.

When we occupied a table at the famous Coffee House off College Street, Rani was easily the star of the show. One day an unknown young man came up to us from another table and started chatting. After a while we asked him to sit down out of politeness. He said, 'No, no, I'll go now. I had taken a bet at our table that I would win five rupees if I showed the guts to come and talk to you.' Such was the star power of Rani Roy.

One day Benu plopped a thick notebook in front of me. I opened it and found Bengali poems written in a neat hand. Benu said to me with a serious face, 'This is the work of the next Rabindranath [Tagore].' I was most impressed. The author of the poems was Shankha Ghosh (b. 1932), who duly emerged as a highly regarded Bengali poet of the second half of the twentieth century.

Almost all my close friends were committed left-wingers in their political views, or at least 'fellow travellers' (sympathisers). This was fairly typical of the educated young generation of West Bengal in those times. Dhriti and Benu were sons of East Bengal zamindar families. Like most people of East Bengal origins dispossessed in one way or another by the Partition of 1947, they disliked the Congress party intensely. My father too was a sympathiser of the Left. The capture of the Congress party in West Bengal after Independence by a small party faction which had been opposed to Subhas and Sarat Bose during the struggle for freedom meant that the progressive sections of the Bengali intelligentsia gravitated towards the Left opposition, particularly the communists. However my own family was not overtly political. My mother was good friends with the freedom fighter and post-independence Congress politician and social worker Phulrenu Guha (1911–2006). Leela Roy *nee* Nag (1900–1970), who was a nationalist revolutionary of the Bose camp, was also known to us. She was from a family of Sylhet district, now in Bangladesh, and had strong Dhaka ties as well. At the same time, the communist leader Jyoti Basu's older sister was also a friend of Mother's through the East Bengal and Dhaka connection.

The left-inclined students of Calcutta in the 1950s were heavily into 'study circles', where profound intellectual discussions would take place. I remember accompanying Dhriti and Benu a few times to one such study circle at the Elgin Road flat of Susobhan Sarkar (1900–1982), who was born into a Brahmo (reformist Hindu) family of Dhaka and became a leading Marxist historian. I remember one particularly intelligent young man from those visits. He was Sukhamoy Chakravarty (1934–1990), a student of economics at Presidency College who would go on to play an important role in the Indian government's Planning Commission. The college was the nursery of a number of superstars of economics. One day I was standing with Bharati, a fellow student, on the first-floor verandah of Presidency College. Bharati asked a group of boys walking below us, 'Do you know where Amartya [Sen] is?' One of the boys looked up and said nonchalantly, 'I guess he is somewhere on *martya* [earth].' Bharati was most annoyed by the flippant response.

Tarak Sen's classes were an experience. He would hold his tutorial classes for MA students in a cubicle by the Presidency library, on the ground floor of the college. We would often begin around 1 pm. The class would continue without a pause through the afternoon.

Late in the afternoon he would give us a tea break. We would rush to the Coffee House and back. Then the session resumed. We were lucky if we got off around 5 pm. Many a time he continued until six or seven in the evening. I remember him teaching us Milton's tragic drama *Samson Agonistes* one evening in the dimly lit corridor. We were exhausted by the time he finished. Someone asked how I felt after the marathon tutorial. I replied with the last line of the play we had just been taught, 'Calm of mind, all passion spent.'

Tarakbabu taught us Milton and Shakespeare, *King Lear* in particular. He also introduced us to Oscar Wilde. I learned the art of literary criticism from him. He used innovative methods to draw us in. One day he brought along a few examples of the work of the English landscape painter Joseph Mallord William Turner (1775–1851). He showed us the prints and asked each of us to pick the one we thought to be the best. Then each of us had to write an essay explaining our choice. My pick was a ship at sea—it was a little blurry, like an out-of-focus photograph. My classmates all picked another one, and Tarakbabu seemed to agree with them. When he returned the essays, I was nervous. Then I saw that he had put the letter 'S' next to what I had written. This stood for 'Satisfactory', considered high praise from Professor Tarak Sen.

Tarakbabu's reserved demeanour concealed a caring heart. This came out in unexpected ways. One day we were at the Coffee House for our brief break during teaching. Benu was having cold coffee with a straw and spotted a foreign object in his cup, which he claimed was a baby cockroach. He decided this was an excellent excuse to skip the rest of the tutorial. When we returned Tarakbabu said quietly, 'I don't see Binod Kishore.' I narrated his mishap as tragically as possible. Tarakbabu became very anxious. He said, 'What! He has swallowed it? Has he taken medicine?' He was so worried that I started to feel guilty. When Benu turned up the next day Professor Sen spent a lot of time fussing over him.

I saw him similarly worried on another occasion. Rani, Benu's sister, had joined a tutorial by special permission. That day she lost her household keys. We wanted to search the cubicle but were too afraid to encroach on Tarakbabu's space after class. Finally the 'three bears' Dhriti, Benu and Arun sent me a.k.a. Goldilocks—his 'favourite student' according to them—to the cubicle. Tarakbabu was a bit surprised to see me. When I explained the problem he stood up in consternation, 'What! Her mother-in-law's keys…' He joined me in rummaging under the table and the bench. No luck. When I emerged from the cubicle Arun was irate with me. He worshipped Professor Sen and felt a man of that stature should not have got on his knees to look for missing keys. But Professor Sen was so taken up with the matter that he instructed us to go to the cleaners' quarters to ask whether they had seen anything.

Because of the length of Tarak Sen's classes at Presidency I would miss some of my classes at Calcutta University. He knew this and cautioned me to maintain the minimum percentage of attendance required. He also gave me advice on which classes were worth attending and which could be given a miss. There was a professor at the university, Srikumarbabu, who students would laugh at because he always spoke ornate and ponderous English. When he saw boys and girls loitering he would say, 'Why are you perpetually perambulating in the corridor?' But Tarak Sen told me to attend Srikumarbabu's classes without fail. He said that Srikumarbabu was an excellent teacher of Romantic literature. Then one day Tarakbabu gave us a thick notebook full of handwritten notes. He told us to copy the notes and return the notebook to him. They were notes Tarakbabu had taken from sitting in on Srikumarbabu's classes.

Professor Tarak Sen's birth centenary was observed in Kolkata in 2009. I am one among countless former students who remember him with awe and affection.

My days at university were not just filled with serious learning. There was plenty of fun too. The boys and girls sat on separate sides of the classroom and addressed one another with the formal '*aapni*' rather than the informal '*tumi*' young people would use today. The *tumi* was reserved for situations where the parties had got to know each other well. One of the professors was a rather harmless man and the boys took liberties with him. They would sit on the side nearest the door, say 'present sir' when he took the roll-call and then depart. He would pretend not to see. One day we girls decided to make things a little difficult for the boys. We went to the class a little in advance and occupied the side near the door. When the boys saw this they quickly devised a counter-strategy. They intercepted the professor in the corridor as he approached and told him that the class had been moved to the next room. He believed them and followed them into the next room, where the boys promptly shut the door. We were stranded outside. After a few minutes of deliberation we knocked on the door. He asked us to come in and take our seats. As we did so the boys erupted in applause. By that point the poor professor had had enough. He cancelled the class for the day and told us all to leave.

Another prank that livened up the classroom was the practice of sticking a piece of paper with something funny written on it on the back of the fellow student sitting at the desk just in front. The girls started this game and the boys soon followed suit in their area of the classroom. I was usually very alert in class and escaped this for a while. Then one day I was absentminded and spent the class staring at the overcast sky through the window. Once the class got over I noticed some of the other students grinning. Then I realised there was something affixed to my back. It read, '*Tumi ki keboli chhobi*!' (Are you just an image!)—the first line of one of Tagore's most haunting songs.

The student union elections came around. Although not as charged as student politics in West Bengal became from the 1960s onwards, it was still a tense moment on campus. My close friend Dhriti Kanta Lahiri Chaudhury, a committed leftist, stood as a candidate. His opponent from the Congress party's student wing was Purnendu, a nice young man, cultured and polite and a poet to boot. One day he gave a campaign speech to our MA group. He spoke looking at the part of the room where the girls were clustered. Someone called out from among the boys, 'Purnendu *bhai* [brother], we're here too!' He was visibly embarrassed. The day before the election I received a one-line letter from Purnendu, 'Tomorrow is election day. I hope to receive your affection.' When I told Dhriti about the missive he was most annoyed, 'What has he written?' I said, 'He wants my affection.' Dhriti said, 'Give him that and give me the vote.'

Dhriti bought a small car, I think it was a car manufactured by the French company Renault. The little Renault greatly increased the mobility of our group of friends. One day the city's public transport went off the roads; the Left opposition parties had called a transport strike. Dhriti arrived at Rashbehari Avenue in his car to drive me to College Street in north Calcutta. While driving we spotted the tall figure of Professor Tarak Nath Sen, umbrella in hand, waiting patiently at a bus stop under a tree. Dhriti stopped and persuaded Professor Sen to take a ride with us. He sat in the front passenger seat and I sat in the back. We were supposed to pick Rani up from her house on Theatre Road (known as Shakespeare Sarani today). When we neared Rani's place I reminded Dhriti, *sotto voce*. He ignored me and drove on. Tarakbabu turned around and said, 'Did you say something?' I replied in the negative. The car stopped at the portico of Presidency College. Tarakbabu disembarked and thanked the chauffeur, 'Dhriti Kanta, you have done me a great favour today.' Then Dhriti turned on me, 'Don't you have any sense? Tarak Sen is riding with us, and you had to mention we have someone else to pick up.' I responded feebly, 'It's abnormal in the city today, I don't think he would have minded.'

This little episode is an example of how deeply we respected our teachers. One day Kajal and I got scolded by Professor Subodh Sengupta for whispering to each other in class, and that too sitting in the front row. He was teaching George Bernard Shaw's play *Arms and the Man*. We were actually talking about the play, because just the previous evening it had been staged in the living room of an old house on Wood Street, close to St. Xavier's School. I had been in the audience. The production was directed by the young Purushottama Lal (1929–2010), known as P. Lal, who was a major figure in Calcutta's literary circles for many decades. Kajal played the female lead and Lal's friend Vishwanathan her lover. In the first scene Vishwanathan entered her bedroom through a real window, exactly as in the play. We tried to apologise to Professor Sengupta after class. He said angrily, 'No you are not sorry!' The boys were quite pleased to see us being ticked off. Arun said, 'You should take my advice before doing things. It would have been better to approach him later.' Arun was right. I ran into Subodh Sengupta on the tram in the early evening. He smiled and said, 'So where are you off to?'

Although I may seem like a pre-historic person to today's young generation, the nature of student life hasn't really changed between the early 1950s and today. We were as carefree and fun-loving then as boys and girls are now. We often went on group jaunts to the restaurants on Park Street. I remember the popular Kwality restaurant had just opened then. On every outing one of us would treat the others. Sometimes we would combine the restaurant outing with a trip to the cinema. Several of Calcutta's old cinemas—Empire, Lighthouse and Globe—were located off Chowringhee, close to Park Street. Benu in particular was a great aficionado of cinema and would often buy tickets for all of us. I remember that on the trip to Kwality it was *Chhorda*'s turn to pay. Chhorda (literally 'younger older brother') was Sanat Bhattacharya, one of our friends. Sanat's older brother was also a student, a bit senior to us in the philosophy department, hence the moniker. Sanat announced during that outing that he intended to join the Indian Administrative Service, the IAS. The idea appealed to Kajal and me and we decided to join him in studying for the IAS examination. For a few days the three of us studied together in the living room of our Rashbehari Avenue flat while

Mother supplied tea and snacks. Thereafter Kajal and I lost our enthusiasm for an IAS career.

The British Council library on Theatre Road was one of our regular haunts. We sat on cane chairs on the verandah around a cane table piled with books. We could talk but at a low volume. Sometimes the conversations breached the tolerable volume level and the British lady at the counter shushed us. After visiting the Council we often walked along Camac Street. The Camac Street–Theatre Road axis is like a '+', where Camac Street is the vertical line and Theatre Road the horizontal line. The lower end of Camac Street connects with Park Street (now Mother Teresa Sarani) and the upper end with the Lower Circular Road (now Acharya

RIGHT: *Krishna's closest university friends. At the British Council, Calcutta (1952)*

Jagadish Chandra Bose Road). In recent decades Camac Street has become lined with shops and offices; the twenty-first-century additions are a mall or two. Back then, sixty years ago, it was a tree-lined street with two-storeyed red-brick residential houses.

Sometimes we would pile into Dhriti's car instead of walking. As the Renault raced along Chowringhee the sky suddenly darkened with storm clouds one evening. Dhriti started to hum a Tagore song, '*Ore jhar neme aaye*' (Come down, o storm). This was the cue for the storm to hit, the big trees on the Maidan swaying wildly in the wind. We admonished Dhriti, who immediately switched to another Tagore song, '*Badal dhara holo shara*' (The rains are spent). This was the cue for a torrential downpour. Soon the roads were flooded with knee-high water. The car broke down on a waterlogged road. An everyday adventure.

Several students slightly senior to us at university became couples in due course. Thus P. Lal married Shyamasree, daughter of the historian Kalidas Nag whose book *Swadesh o Sabhyata* (Our Land and Civilisation) was such an influence on me in my adolescence. I know Shyamasree Lal as Kisha, another of her names. There were others—Rubydi married Nirupamda. There were no couplings among our close-knit group of friends but the friendships were for life. After our university years we went our separate ways and rarely met each other. But Kajal, Rani, Dhriti, Benu, Arun, Sanat and I remained linked by a deep, unspoken connection all our lives.

As our MA classes drew to a close after two wonderful years we made a trip in Dhriti's car to Diamond Harbour, a pretty rural area just south of Calcutta by the bank of the Hooghly river, not too far short of where the river flows into the Bay of Bengal. We got into a boat at Diamond Harbour—the river is very wide there and the expanse of water stretches almost as far as the eye can see. Dhriti had brought along a single-bore hunting rifle. The scion of a zamindar family, he was trained in marksmanship. He downed eleven birds with twelve shots from the boat. The birds hit the water with a 'jhup' sound, sometimes with a faint trail of blood. Local lads sitting on the bank dived into the water to recover them for the *shikari* (hunter). After a while I covered my eyes with *The Statesman* newspaper. The hunting game was not for me.

The bird shooting over, we adjourned to the bank. The bank was dotted with *khejur* trees (date palms) and the locals gave us fresh date-palm juice. I refused for fear of becoming intoxicated. Kajal bravely sipped the juice from a rather dirty glass. The conversation turned to the names of our future children. Kajal said, 'I really like your name; I'm going to name my daughter Krishna.' Rani, who had got married early, already had a little daughter, Bubli. We all doted on her. How about Dhriti's future progeny? His father, grandfather and great-grandfather all had names like Dhirendra Kanta, Dharani Kanta and so on. He speculated that he could name his son Dhappabaj Kanta or Dharibaj Kanta. In colloquial Bengali, a *dhappabaj* is a cheat or fraud and a *dharibaj* a crafty schemer.

As it turned out, Dhriti and his wife Sheila's son got a very nice name: Deep Kanta. Benu married Sumitra and they had two daughters. Arun and his wife also had two daughters. Kajal went to Oxford for further studies in English and married later than the rest of us. When she returned she joined Presidency College as one of its first women faculty. On her first day of teaching some of her male students scrawled on the blackboard, '*Maa-go amar sholokbola Kajla-didi koi*?' (O mother, where is my verse-spouting Kajla-didi). She achieved great popularity as a teacher at Presidency in the course of her long career there.

I managed to continue my freelance writing alongside the classes and the hectic social life. I mentioned at the beginning of this chapter that I had developed an interest in modern art. I sent an article titled '*Adhunik Chitrakala*' (Modern Art) to *Desh*, the leading Bengali magazine of literature and criticism. Sagarmoy Ghosh, the editor, liked it and it was published. Greatly encouraged, I sent a follow-up piece. Those were my first two published articles in

Bengali. Though I did not know it at the time, it was the beginning of a long relationship with Sagarmoy Ghosh. Much later, two of my books on Netaji's life were serialised in *Desh* and then published as books. The first was *Itihaser Sandhane* (In Search of History), on Netaji's time in Europe during the 1930s and in the early 1940s. This came out in the early 1970s. Nearly a decade later I wrote *Charanarekha Taba* (In His Footsteps), on Netaji in Southeast Asia between 1943 and 1945.

Meanwhile a new English evening paper—*Free Lance*—appeared in Calcutta. Its editors asked me to cover the city's art exhibitions for them. My pieces were anonymous: 'By our art critic.' At that point I was set on a career as an art critic. Father's library was a most useful resource for building up my knowledge.

Then all of a sudden I got an offer to be a film critic as well! Chanchal Sarkar, a distant maternal uncle, returned from studies in England and joined the editorial staff of *The Statesman*. He offered me the vacant position of the paper's film critic. It was really tempting. *The Statesman* was one of India's most reputable newspapers at that time. But after consideration I said no. I just didn't have the time to watch a movie most days of the week.

So I stayed with art criticism. The leading artist Paritosh Sen (1918–2008), a founding member of the 1940s 'Calcutta Group' of artists with Gopal Ghose and others, liked my piece on one of his exhibitions and wrote a nice letter to the editor. He referred to me as 'he'. Uncle Nirad mentioned in one of his letters from Delhi that he was receiving free copies of a new evening daily being published in Calcutta. He said he found it rather ordinary, but the art critic's pieces were not bad. I was elated and informed him of the writer's identity. He wrote in his next letter that he was impressed with how well I had picked up French—one of my pieces had had a long quotation in that language.

At that time Abani C. Banerji was a well-known figure in the art world of Calcutta. He invited me to give a public lecture on modern art. Initially the venue of the lecture was supposed to be

Netaji Bhawan on Elgin Road, but that didn't work out for some reason. So I gave the first public lecture of my life at the YMCA Hall on Chowringhee. It went well—I gave a talk using slides. Soumen Tagore (1910–1974), a leading communist intellectual and a scion of the Tagore family, was among the audience. At the end of the talk the film critic Chidananda Dasgupta (1921–2011) took a copy of the lecture. He used to work then for *Amrita Bazar Patrika*, the long-established English daily of Calcutta known for its steadfast support of the freedom struggle in the colonial period. The text was published in the paper the next day.

Around this time I took my examination for the *sangeet visharad* title in sitar. The examiner who came down from Lucknow was the young Pandit V.G. Jog (1922–2004), who achieved fame for introducing the violin into Hindustani classical music. I hadn't practised much but I passed.

My favourite retreat during my university years was the Ramakrishna Mission Institute of Culture. At that time the Institute did not occupy its sprawling campus in Golpark in the heart of south Kolkata—this was built in 1960. It was based in a donated three-storey building in Tollygunge, an area in the city's southern suburbs. I used to attend lectures there. Nitya Swarupanandaji was in charge. I met many of the speakers, including Swami Akhilananda and Swami Nikhilananda. They were both based in the United States then but were from the Mymensingh district of East Bengal and knew my father's family.

Today several of India's political leaders, from Narendra Modi to Mamata Banerjee, cite Swami Vivekananda—the mystic Ramakrishna Paramahansa's most famous disciple who founded the Ramakrishna Mission in 1897—as their idol and inspiration. I too was influenced by Vivekananda's philosophy from childhood, after reading some of his works in Father's library. Father was atheist all his life but he admired the Mission's commitment to serve and uplift the poor, the needy and the downtrodden. He also knew some of the monks of the Ramakrishna order, especially those of East

Bengal origins. My parents would join me on trips to Tollygunge at times. They both knew Swami Abhayananda (Bharat Maharaj) who for decades headed the Ramakrishna Mission's headquarters at Belur Math in Howrah, just across the Hooghly river from the northern outskirts of Calcutta. The philosophy of Ramakrishna and Vivekananda was a huge influence on Subhas Chandra Bose as well, and my marriage to Netaji's nephew Sisir Kumar Bose at the end of 1955 reinforced my lifelong connection to that fount of Indian spirituality and selfless service.

The topic of spirituality reminds me of Premananda, the monk I briefly alluded to towards the end of the last chapter. Of East Bengal origin, he was a student at Calcutta's Presidency College when he embraced asceticism. He spent most of his life living and meditating in the mountains of Kashmir. When the raiders from Pakistan struck at the Kashmir Valley in late 1947 he finally abandoned his Himalayan refuge. By then he was an elderly man. He knew my maternal grandfather Lalit Roy well since childhood years in East Bengal. On a visit to Calcutta he heard that my grandmother was still living and came to see her.

Cheats, frauds, even rapists have given Indian godmen a very bad name. The outrightly criminal types aside, a highly commercialised godman industry exists. It existed even back then. Premananda preferred a low-profile existence. He was averse to publicity, and he did not build an ashram anywhere. He spent the last decade of his life—which is when we knew him—travelling between Agra, Benares, Calcutta, Darjeeling and Puri, among other places. Nor did he aggressively pursue disciples, and he did not formally baptise devotees (*deeksha*). He met my mother through my grandmother. During their conversation he inquired, 'How many children do you have?' Mother replied, 'I have one daughter.' He smiled and said, 'How can you be so foolish, Ma? You have one son and one daughter.' In Bengal it's usual to refer to daughters and daughter-like persons as Ma, as a term of endearment.

Once Premananda appointed himself as her son—purely honorary of course, and in a manner of speaking—my mother became hopelessly devoted to him. A revolutionary development then took place in our household in my early adulthood. None of our addresses had ever had a puja or thakur ghar found in millions of Indian homes—a room or area designated for worship adorned with idols of deities and images of gurus. This was due to Father's strongly atheist beliefs, which had its roots in the sceptical and reformist views of his Brahmo Samajist mother. Now Mother established a small *thakurer asan* (seat for the gods) in a corner of our Rashbehari Avenue flat, with pictures of Premananda as well as idols and images of a few other deities such as Lord Krishna. Father showed no interest but did not object.

Partly due to Mother's nagging and partly out of curiosity I agreed to meet Swamiji. The first meeting consisted mostly of discussions of English literature. I was impressed by the elderly monk's razor-sharp memory—he recited entire passages from Shakespeare's plays faultlessly. He was also an expert in Sanskrit. In the 1930s he had published an original collection of devotional verses and hymns (puja mantra) based on his reading of the *Upanishads*, the ancient Vedic texts. Gopinath Kaviraj, a religious scholar of Benares, had helped him. The idea was to dispense with the services of professional priests. Instead a family or community could perform their own puja (worship) using the book of verses and hymns.

Once I was converted, it was Father's turn. He held out. It took a lot of persuasion by me to get him to agree to a meeting with Swami Premananda. When they met, the monk told Father, 'I like atheists. They are far better people than false believers.' Father was charmed. Father was an exponent of the esraj, a harp-like string instrument popular in Bengal (the north Indian version is called the *dilruba*). Whenever Swamiji came to Calcutta after that Father would visit him, esraj in hand. I would sing devotional music while Father accompanied me on the esraj and Shashi Bhushan

Dasgupta, a professor at Calcutta University, played the *khol*, a two-sided terracotta drum which is hollow inside.

Discussions and even polite arguments would take place during these sessions. Father was not convinced of the need to believe in God. Why is there so much grief in the world if an Almighty exists, he would ask Swamiji. Swamiji would respond that human existence is a complicated interplay of positive and negative elements. One must strive to be happy nonetheless, and faith helps. One of his favourite utterances was, 'A storm strengthens the tree, as long as the tree is able to keep standing.' During my life I have realised that faith does help to cope with adversity and distress, it helps one to keep standing and become more resilient. Faith assists, in the words of my favourite English poet, Robert Browning, 'the search of the finite soul for the infinite'.

The MA examinations approached. Classes had ended and everyone was busy studying at home. At this time I suddenly had a meltdown of self-confidence, to this day not really explicable even to myself. I announced that I was not sufficiently prepared so would not sit the examinations. Father was away at a Speakers' Conference in Gwalior; I hadn't gone because of the imminent exams. Uncle Khirode, the paediatrician, turned up on hearing of my decision. He said to me, 'What's the worst that can happen? You'll fail. Then we will get you married.' I tearfully replied, 'If I fail no one will marry me.' He responded, 'Why not? We will find a failed boy if necessary.' He prescribed daily chicken soup and a tonic and disappeared.

Kajal and my other friends tried very hard to persuade me to see sense. P. Lal lived in a flat on Southern Avenue. One day there was a get-together of friends on the roof of his building. Lal took me aside at one point and said, 'Don't do this. You won't fail even if you try.'

Nothing doing. Father returned from Gwalior. He was thoroughly exasperated with me but didn't know what to do.

Free of exam preparations, I would join him on his leisurely morning walks along the lakes close to our Rashbehari Avenue home. One morning we ran into Professor Subodh Sengupta. He was surprised to see me strolling without a care in the world and ordered me to go home immediately and start studying. I stopped going to the lakes for fear of encountering him again.

Then one day I went to visit my maternal grandmother, who was confined to bed due to old age and illness. She lived in a flat on Theatre Road, just opposite the British Council building. The flat had belonged to Uncle Kiran. There was no one else around. As I sat by her bed she took my hand in hers and said in a tone of affectionate concern, 'What's happened to you? Why have you given up your studies?'

On the way home my grandmother's words kept echoing in my head, 'What's happened to you? You were always so good at your studies.' When I got home I retrieved my books from the shelf, dusted them off and sat down to study. Father and Mother pretended not to notice and said nothing. They were probably apprehensive that I might change my mind yet again.

At that point there were eight days left for the start of the examinations. We had to sit eight papers in all. I started with the eighth paper and studied for one paper each day, ending with the first paper the day before the exams began. In the examination hall I was fine. When the results came out Kajal ranked first in the university and Arun came second. I was joint third with another student, a boy.

Kajal departed for Oxford on a scholarship awarded by the West Bengal state government. Arun went to Oxford the following year. I set out to look for a lecturing job in Calcutta, carrying a recommendation written by Professor Tarak Sen. The letter mentioned among other things that I came from a highly educated and cultured family background. My first successful application was to Muralidhar College, a small college for women on Hindustan Road, very close to where I had spent my childhood years on Dover Lane. I met the principal, Nalini Mohan Shastri, and he took me on as a temporary teacher for a month. It wasn't much but that first experience of teaching greatly increased my self-confidence.

Had Mother had her way I would probably have been married off after passing my matriculation examinations, as so many girls of my background and social class were. Father was insistent that I must receive and complete higher education before marriage would even be considered. Now that I had started to look for employment Father said, 'What's the need? You can write, do your art critic stuff—isn't that enough?' Mother put her foot down. She said, 'She has put in a lot of effort to earn the educational qualifications she has. She should work if she wants to.'

I heard that Roma Choudhury, the principal of Lady Brabourne College—a premier women's college of Calcutta—was looking for me. She had found out that I was the author of the critique of the factory production line nature of higher education published under the pseudonym 'Roll Number 13' in *The Statesman* a few years earlier. We had a nice conversation and I liked her very much. As I rose to leave she asked, 'Are you interested in teaching?' When I nodded she told me that one of her teaching staff was going on leave for two months. I received the appointment letter to the 'leave vacancy' position the next day.

At that time college education consisted of four years: two years of 'Intermediate' studies followed by another two years for the bachelor's degree. The students in the 'fourth year' were only a little younger than me. I would walk into the fourth-year classroom mustering as much gravitas as possible, the attendance register in my hand. Romadi, a very noted educationist of the city, would patrol the corridors at times. She liked to keep a watch on the goings-on in the college. She noticed that the students paid attention to my teaching and told me so. She also said, 'Teaching is an art. Not everyone can do it.'

My duties at Lady Brabourne College went beyond formal teaching. At the annual cultural programme the students performed Tagore's dance-drama *Shyama*. I played the sitar as one of the accompanying musicians. I remember a lot of rehearsals went into this event. Then there was the weekly guest speaker series. Every Wednesday, at 4 pm, a guest speaker would give a talk to the students. One week a leading physician spoke on tuberculosis, another week a scholar of Bengal's folk music spoke on the *baul*s, the wandering minstrels of the Bengal countryside. I would introduce the speaker, say a few words on the topic of the day, and deliver the vote of thanks at the end. I realised later what a valuable experience it was.

The two months went by fast and my temporary position ended. Romadi didn't forget me and several years later she offered me a permanent position. By that time I was permanently employed elsewhere. Life had moved on.

A NEW LIFE

1955 was a transformative year in my life, on both personal and professional fronts. The year brought me a stable career on the one hand and my life partner on the other.

Six decades ago most women of my social class with higher education did not pursue a career after completing their studies. But I was determined to stand on my own feet, to have an independent means of livelihood.

The 'City College' network was well-known in Calcutta's higher education sphere. It was a cluster of colleges with campuses in north Calcutta, on Amherst Street and College Street. A new City College campus—City College South—opened on Golpark in the heart of south Calcutta, walking distance from our home on Rashbehari Avenue. I applied for a teaching job there.

The interview took place on the Amherst Street site. It was a very serious occasion. A bevy of senior professors—all male—sat stern-faced around a large horseshoe-shaped table. I was quizzed for quite a while. One elderly professor was reclining in an armchair. He asked searching questions about the work of Christopher Marlowe, the sixteenth-century English playwright and poet. I later learned he was Professor Amiya Sen. Another member of the interview panel, Professor P.C. Ghosh, asked no questions at all. I had taken MA classes with him at Calcutta University, where he always lectured with his eyes half-closed. When queried if he

ABOVE: *Krishna—a portrait (1955)*

wanted to ask anything he replied, eyes half-closed as always, 'No, I know her. She was my student.' The interview was challenging and I wasn't confident of the outcome. But a few days later the appointment letter arrived in the post. In July I started work at Sivanath Sastri College, the new college for women on the City College consortium's south Calcutta campus. It is named after the Brahmo Samajist reformer and scholar Sivanath Sastri (1847–1919).

The teaching career I began that day lasted forty years, until my retirement at the end of 1995. During those four decades I served for many years as Head of the Department of English. Then in 1983 I received an unexpected responsibility. Sisir and I had gone to Britain and the United States for a few weeks over my summer vacation in May–June. When I returned I found that I had been appointed Principal of Sivanath Sastri College by the governing body of the City Colleges following the retirement of the previous incumbent. I was initially reluctant to take on the job of administering the college, which had grown a lot in size and complexity since my early years there. I went to the Rector of the City Colleges, Professor Arun Sen, and told him I wanted to stay with teaching and writing. I was also apprehensive about having to deal with the rising interference of political parties in higher education. Professor Sen persuaded me to give it a shot, and assured me of full support whenever difficulties arose.

My seven years as principal (1983–1990) were full of difficult moments but the challenges also made for a very instructive and rewarding experience. The 1980s was the decade when the Communist Party of India (Marxist) or CPI(M)—the party that ruled West Bengal at the head of the Left Front from 1977 to 2011—imposed a vice-like grip on the state's colleges and universities. Of course, they were not unique in this regard. During the time I was a Member of Parliament in the Lok Sabha, elements of the Hindu nationalist *sangh-parivar* (family of organisations) made efforts to 'saffronise' education, especially during the 1999–2004 coalition government in New Delhi headed by the Bharatiya Janata Party (BJP). I had been elected to that Lok Sabha standing for the recently born Trinamool Congress (TMC), which was a constituent of the ruling coalition. Nonetheless, in a debate in Parliament I opposed and warned against the 'saffronisation' agenda. I pointed out that the CPI(M) had spread its tentacles throughout the education system of my state and almost literally painted it red. The quality of education had been ruined and the integrity of the teaching community all but destroyed in the process. Education must remain autonomous of political influence, I argued. Its colour must remain pure white, and not become red or saffron or anything else.

My strong views were derived from real experiences. As the chief administrator of my college I had to recurrently deal with student agitations fomented by political parties. On many occasions I was gherao-d in my office—surrounded by agitators and not allowed to leave. Various political parties were complicit but the CPI(M)-backed students were the most systematic in the way they went about spreading their influence. By comparison the students of the Congress's student wing, the *Chhatra Parishad*, were disorganised. The CPI(M)'s Students' Federation of India (SFI) used all sorts of tactics. During one gherao a boy activist of the SFI—who shouldn't have been agitating on the campus of a girls' college, let alone inside my office—leaned forward and presented his cheek to me. He said, 'Madam, please slap me.' I replied, 'Don't tempt me.'

One particular experience is etched in my memories. I was slightly unwell and had taken a day's leave. As fate would have it, in mid-morning I received an SOS phone call at home, 'Please come immediately. The Congress leader Subrata Mukherjee has entered the college and is giving a speech with a handheld loudspeaker on the lawns.' Our driver hadn't come to work so I got into a taxi and rushed there. I came face to face with Subrata, a known firebrand in those days, and Mamata Banerjee, who was with him. I told them calmly, 'You are causing a disturbance. Classes are going on. Please leave the campus immediately.' They meekly complied.

Subrata was then the Chief Whip of the Opposition in the West Bengal Legislative Assembly and my husband Sisir was a Congress MLA (Member of the Legislative Assembly) elected from Calcutta's Chowringhee constituency. Subrata told Sisir in the Assembly that afternoon, 'We had gone to Boudi's college today. She threw us out.' Mamata was then a virtually unknown, young activist—this was before she was elected to the Lok Sabha for the first time in December 1984 from Jadavpur, the Greater Calcutta constituency I would later represent for three terms in the Lok Sabha. But I knew her well because she had campaigned energetically in Sisir's election from Chowringhee in 1982. Subrata and Mamata are still comrades-in-arms—he is a senior cabinet minister in her government in West Bengal.

A handful of my academic colleagues, mostly men, started a whisper campaign after this incident that I had been aware in advance and deliberately not come to work that day. But my students' union—dominated by girls belonging to the SFI and the Progressive Students' Union (PSU), the student wing of a smaller Left Front constituent, the Revolutionary Socialist Party or RSP—stood by me. They declared that they had full confidence in me. The crisis passed.

Looking back, I realise that the respect of countless students is by far the greatest reward of my academic career. Even today, former students come up and introduce themselves on the streets, at public events, and even on flights. Some are now themselves of advanced age. During my four Lok Sabha campaigns I ran into large numbers of former students in my parliamentary constituency in southern Calcutta and its suburbs. I was touched by their goodwill.

Just after Obama won the United States presidency in November 2008 a middle-aged woman approached me at a public gathering. She introduced herself as a former student and said, 'When Obama won I thought of you.' I was perplexed. She explained that I had taught her class a play about Abraham Lincoln's life. That was how she came to know of slavery and racism in modern America.

Some of the young fellow teachers I met during my first days at work remained my colleagues for decades thereafter. They included Reba Rudra in the Sanskrit Department, Jayati Sengupta in History and Neeti Banerjee in Philosophy. Neeti's husband was a freedom fighter who had been jailed in the Andaman Islands; post-independence he was an activist of the Communist Party of India (CPI). A few years later a remarkable and inspiring woman joined the faculty—Ila Mitra (1925–2002). Born into an elite family of Calcutta, Ila Mitra became involved in organising peasant struggles in rural Bengal in 1946–1947 after marrying a progressive zamindar. After the August 1947 Partition she stayed on in East Bengal and continued to mobilise poor peasants, especially from the tribal Santhal community. In early 1950 she led a peasant uprising in East Bengal's Rajshahi district, close to the border with West Bengal. The uprising was brutally crushed and she endured savage torture in the custody of the Pakistani police and military. She came back to Calcutta in 1954 and continued her political activities as a CPI leader. She was elected to West Bengal's legislative assembly four times from a north Calcutta constituency in the 1960s and 1970s. I was very good friends with Iladi. I was also friendly with another communist colleague, Divya Narayan Bhattacharya, who was active in Calcutta's theatre world and taught in the Bengali Department. The Bengali Department also had Bhaskar Mitra, a talented musician. A close friend, he died tragically early.

During the latter half of my career we branched out from the traditional liberal arts and introduced an Honours course in Commerce for our students. Society was gradually changing and more and more young women sought employment after graduation.

The Commerce programme provided an employment-friendly degree. Many of our Commerce recruits were extremely bright girls who would obtain first-class marks in the university examinations. Many succeeded in the job market and went on to professional success. Today Sivanath Sastri College is rated as one of India's top fifty colleges for studying commerce.

I began my career in July 1955 and in August my marriage was finalised—to Sisir Kumar Bose, a young doctor, a son of Sarat Chandra Bose and nephew of Netaji Subhas Chandra Bose. The wedding took place three months later, in December 1955. During those three months we had chaperoned meetings many times—sometimes at family dinners, sometimes at the Rashbehari Avenue residence of the photographer Sunil Janah and his wife Shobhadi, my maternal cousin, and sometimes at the house of my paternal uncle, Khirode C. Chaudhuri, like Sisir a paediatrician with lots of training in Europe. Uncle Khirode lived in a house on Creek Row in central Calcutta with his second wife Amala. Occasionally he would tell Aunt Amala to invite us over when he was out of town; he felt we might be more relaxed in his absence.

I had noticed that Sisir had a reserved personality and spoke little. As Sisir and I sat on the south-facing verandah of the Creek Row house after dinner one night, he surprised me by opening up. That night I learned of a side of his life and personality that had been completely unknown to me. I had thought I was marrying a smart young paediatrician embarking, like me, on his professional career after completing advanced training in Britain and

BELOW: *Krishna and Sisir before their wedding (October 1955). Photograph courtesy of Sunil Janah*

continental Europe. That night I learned of his central role in Netaji's historic escape from India in 1941, when Sisir had helped plan the escape and driven his uncle in the dead of night from the Bose family house on Calcutta's Elgin Road to the Gomoh rail junction in Bihar (now in Jharkhand). I learned of his daring underground activities on behalf of Netaji from 1941 to 1944, which led to his arrest and imprisonment first in the Red Fort in Delhi and then for a longer spell in solitary confinement in the Lahore Fort. I had had no idea that my husband-to-be had such an interesting past.

And that past shaped our life together for decades, for nearly forty-five years till Sisir's death on 30 September 2000. Sisir had been very deeply influenced by his association with Netaji's struggle for India's freedom. Netaji told his Austrian wife Emilie Schenkl quite frankly that his country was his first and only love. I once told Subhas and Emilie's only child, my sister-in-law Anita Bose Pfaff, that although Sisir was never so explicit with me about his priorities it rapidly became clear to me that my husband's life was charged with a commitment to preserve Netaji's memory and the legacy of his life and struggle for the people and the future generations of independent India. I decided early on to help and support him in this endeavour.

In the process I discovered that Subhas Chandra Bose was much more than a romantic hero or a swashbuckling action-figure. After our marriage I read his 'Haripura address' with Sisir. This is the presidential address Netaji gave at the annual convention of the Indian National Congress in 1938. The convention was held at Haripura, a village in Gujarat's Surat district on the banks of the Tapti river. Netaji was anointed Congress president there, and a year later in 1939 he won re-election to the post by defeating Gandhi's preferred nominee in a nationwide ballot of All India Congress Committee (AICC) members. The Haripura address is a clear and sophisticated analysis of India's problems and proposes concrete solutions after independence. It is the speech of a revolutionary statesman. I read it in page-proof form before it went for printing in the publication series of the Netaji Research Bureau, the institution established by Sisir in 1957 at Calcutta's Netaji Bhawan.

Sisir's mission to document Netaji's life and work as a priceless legacy for India's people and future generations was difficult. Those in the corridors of power in both Calcutta and New Delhi were indifferent and sometimes hostile, so official support was not forthcoming as it should have. There was also a logistical problem even a big team of researchers would have found daunting. Netaji's life crossed continents and traversed the globe. He had spent a lot of time in Europe during the 1930s and in the early 1940s. And the climactic phase of his struggle to liberate India was based in the countries of Southeast Asia between 1943 and 1945. Sisir worked painstakingly over many years to piece together all the periods and elements of Netaji's life by building contacts with Netaji's comrades in struggle, friends and acquaintances throughout the subcontinent and all over the world, and by slowly gathering a vast array of materials including letters and other documents, photographs and footage. A prime selection of this treasure-trove of material is presented in the Netaji Bhawan's world-class museum, which Sisir established in the early 1960s and gradually built up.

This work was in addition to his increasingly busy professional life as a paediatrician. By joining him in his work on Netaji I gained a lot of insight into India's struggle for freedom. In 1971 we travelled to a number of countries in Europe to meet Netaji's associates, scholars, and of course Netaji's wife Emilie at her home in Vienna. After we returned, I wrote an account based on our travels of Netaji in Europe—*Itihaser Sandhane* (In Search of History)—which was first serialised in the magazine *Desh* by its editor Sagarmoy Ghosh and then released as a book. Its success encouraged me to write a sequel of sorts. In 1979 Sisir and I travelled to Japan as well as Taiwan and several Southeast Asian countries—Singapore, Malaysia, Thailand—on another research trip. After that I wrote *Charanarekha Taba* (In His Footsteps), an account of the climactic phase of Netaji's struggle from 1943 to 1945. This too was first serialised in *Desh* and then published as a book.

In October 1955 the annual conference of the Speakers of the Vidhan Sabhas was held in Shillong, a picturesque hill town in Assam (in 1972 it became the capital of the state of Meghalaya, carved out of Assam). I accompanied Father and Mother there. At the conference the news of my impending marriage became widely known to attendees from across India. The wedding preparations began in earnest as soon as we returned from Shillong to Calcutta.

The wedding invitation card was simple, decorated with *alpana* motifs taken from the work of Abanindranath Tagore. Alpana is a form of decorative art of Bengal using a mixture of rice powder and water which is typically drawn on floors on festive and holy days. Alpana is especially associated with the worship of female deities (goddesses) in Bengal. The card was decorated with footprints of the Goddess Lakshmi and with the lotus flower among other motifs. Uncle Nirad's sons Dhruva and Kirti arrived from Delhi. Dhruva was armed with a movie camera and captured my beautiful friend Rani opening the invitation. My university classmates were all very excited. In one of the Bengali wedding rituals, the bride is carried in seven circular motions while seated on a *piri* (a very low stool) around the stationary groom. Dhriti and Benu formed a 'carrying committee' which carefully researched details such as my weight and determined who would lift and hold me from different sides. Dhriti has always had a great sense of humour. He told me, 'It would have been better if your husband was a dermatologist and not a paediatrician.' He explained that skin diseases are difficult to cure so the patients stay with the doctor for a long time, if not forever. Moreover a paediatrician would have to run night or day to attend to a patient whenever an anxious parent got spooked by a crying child.

The sprawling compound of Tripura Bhavan on south Calcutta's Ballygunge Circular Road had two elegant mansions. One was rented out for weddings. This was chosen as the venue of my marriage to Sisir on the evening of 9 December 1955. The date had a special significance: Sisir's father Sarat Bose had got married to his mother Bivabati on 9 December 1910. A shamiana—a large rectangular canopy with a colourful cloth roof—was put up in the garden for the guests to mingle. In a room of the house I got appropriately bedecked in bridal attire. Monuadi, the beautiful daughter of our neighbours in my childhood home on Dover Lane, was in charge. Lady Ranu Mookerjee, my classmate from French lessons, arrived early. She kept a close watch as Monuadi supervised my bridal costume and make-up.

The guests were an eclectic collection. There were politicians and administrators whom Father knew through work. Then there were his friends from the world of culture. Of course Father's close

RIGHT: *Krishna and Sisir's wedding, Calcutta (December 1955). Krishna's uncle Benode C. Chaudhuri (with glasses) is in the centre*

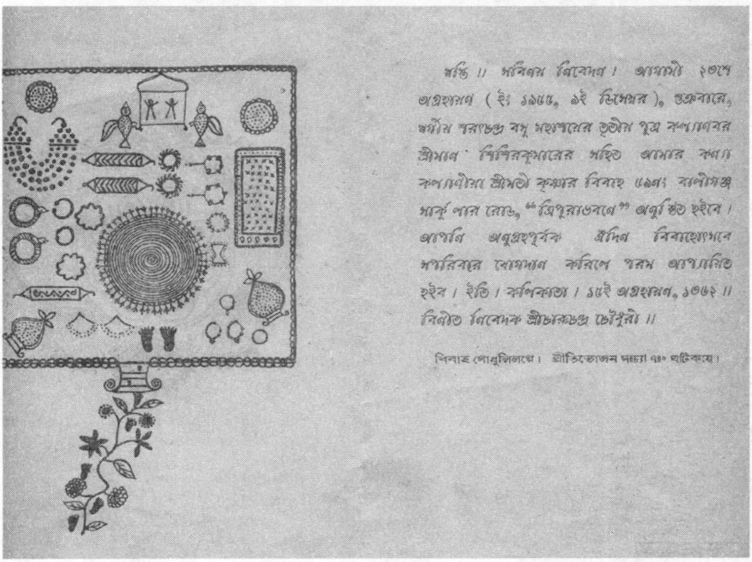

স্বস্তি ॥ সবিনয় নিবেদন। আগামী ২৩শে অগ্রহায়ণ (ইং ১৯৫৫, ৯ই ডিসেম্বর), শুক্রবারে, স্বর্গীয় শরৎচন্দ্র বসু মহাশয়ের তৃতীয় পুত্র কল্যাণবর শ্রীমান শিশিরকুমারের সহিত আমার কন্যা কল্যাণীয়া শ্রীমতী কৃষ্ণার বিবাহ এবং বালীগঞ্জ সার্কুলার রোড, "ত্রিপুরাভবনে" অনুষ্ঠিত হইবে। আপনি অনুগ্রহপূর্বক ঐদিন বিবাহোৎসবে সপরিবারে যোগদান করিলে পরম আপ্যায়িত হইব। ইতি। কলিকাতা। ১৫ই অগ্রহায়ণ, ১৩৬২ ॥ বিনীত নিবেদক শ্রীচারুচন্দ্র চৌধুরী ॥

বিবাহ গোধূলিলগ্নে। প্রীতিভোজন সন্ধ্যা ৭॥০ ঘটিকায়।

ABOVE: *Krishna and Sisir's* shubhodrishti *—a ritual in Bengali marriages, literally meaning 'auspicious sight' (1955)*

LEFT: *Krishna and Sisir's wedding invitation (1955)*

friend Phani Bhushan Chakraborty, who had seen me grow up since early childhood, was present. He was then the chief justice of the Calcutta high court. The linguist Suniti Kumar Chatterji brought a copy of the Mahabharata, the ancient Indian epic, as a gift. The writer-couple Narendra Dev and Radharani Devi, our neighbours

on Rashbehari Avenue, brought copies of their own books as gifts. Another family friend and neighbour, the hard-drinking artist Gopal Ghose, was hard at work decorating the area where the wedding rituals would take place in alpana style. Atul Bose, the portrait specialist, arrived bearing a special gift—a painting by the celebrated artist Jamini Roy.

Sisir, a man of sober tastes, had told my family that the car sent to bring him from his home—1 Woodburn Park, the house his father had built in the 1920s on Woodburn Road, just off Elgin Road—to the wedding venue should not have the usual floral decoration. So my maternal uncle Suren Roy's Chevrolet—a big vehicle, as American cars invariably were at that time—was dispatched there sans any make-up. Sisir had also sent word that he wouldn't sit on a throne-like chair as Indian bridegrooms usually do. So a simple rug was spread on the ground. As the groom's arrival approached my *shaj ghar* (dressing room) filled up with women, including several of my new work colleagues. Uncle Khirode was in charge of greeting the guests and the members of the groom's family. Another of Father's brothers, Uncle Hiranmoy, supervised the cooks in the kitchen set up on the premises to prepare the wedding feast. The sweets to follow the main meal were also being prepared on site by a team of expert makers of Bengali desserts, in a sweet-making kitchen known as the *vien*. Father's youngest brother, Uncle Benode, had been entrusted with the *sampradaan*—the ritual of formally giving away the bride to the groom and his family. Uncle Benode took this very seriously and had fasted all day in keeping with tradition. Uncle Manmatha, another of my paternal uncles, teased his younger brother relentlessly. Uncle Benode was known for his fiery temper and Uncle Manmatha guessed the fasting might keep him quiet, 'Let us starve the lion,' he said.

Then a cry went up: '*Bor eshechhe!*' (The groom has arrived). My dressing room emptied as everyone ran to see the groom. As I sat alone Anil kaka—Anil Ganguly, a barrister and a close friend of Father's—appeared. He had had a glimpse of the groom and

FACING PAGE: *Krishna and Sisir, 12 December 1955*

ABOVE: *Krishna and Sisir's wedding (December 1955). Pandit Gauri Nath Shastri is in the background (on the left)*

sang the first line of a Bengali song which described the man he had just seen as God's chosen one. It was a touching moment. Outside I could hear the *shehnai* musicians—the flute-players who traditionally provide the background music at Indian weddings—competing with the Calcutta police band's rendition of a popular patriotic song.

The wedding was conducted by Pandit Gauri Nath Shastri, the family priest of the Bose family. He beautifully recited the Sanskrit verses sanctifying our union; as someone proficient in Sanskrit I could appreciate just how good he was. Occasionally he paused to explain the meaning of the verses to the assembled guests, in Bengali and in English. 'May you reside like a shining star in your husband's home,' one blessing went. Amid the Sanskrit intonations, the soulful evening melodies of the shehnai, and the tunes of patriotic music by the band I began a new life.

My new life left many addresses behind—the little house off Chowringhee of my earliest memories, the houses on Dover Lane where I was thrilled by fox cries later in my childhood, the wide expanse of Rashbehari Avenue lined with purple *jarul* and blazing-red *krishnachura* trees where I spent my adolescence and early adulthood. Other addresses full of happy vacation memories were left behind as well—the house called Balaclava in Ghoom near Darjeeling, the house called Benubon at Mihijam in the Santhal Parganas. That's normal—life moves on. Yet looking back, I realise that those lost addresses gave me an interesting start to life. My personal and familial story of those beginnings is intertwined with the story of Calcutta, Bengal and India at a time of historic transition.

ACKNOWLEDGEMENTS

I have the habit of keeping a diary since childhood. An old, tattered diary was indispensable to writing this memoir.

My older son, Sugata, constantly encouraged me. My younger son, Sumantra, motivated me when I was writing in 2012–2013 by giving me his own book manuscript to read.

Others who provided assistance of various kinds are Kartik Chakraborty, Sukhamay Choudhury, Manohar Mandal, Anirban Bhattacharjee, and Mou Banerjee. Amala Singh and Rakhahari Mahato looked after the household at 90 Sarat Bose Road, Kolkata.

The photographs in this book were taken by Parimal Goswami, William Pereira, Charu Chandra Chaudhuri, Dhruva Narayan Chaudhuri, Sumantra Bose, and myself. Subir Mitra and his colleagues at Ananda Publishers, Kolkata, took the initiative to publish the book in the Bengali original. I am grateful to everyone at Niyogi Books, Delhi, especially the editor, Sucharita Ghosh, for bringing out the English edition.

